Can the Working Class Change the World?

CAN THE WORKING CLASS CHANGE THE WORLD?

MICHAEL D. YATES

MONTHLY REVIEW PRESS

New York

Library of Congress Cataloging-in-Publication Data
available from the publisher

ISBN paper: 978-1-58367-710-0
ISBN cloth: 978-1-58367-711.7

Our thanks to The Labor Heritage Foundation's Fasanella Public Domain
Project, which raises funds to purchase original Fasanella paintings and
place them in museums and public buildings: www.fasanella.org.

Typeset in Minion Pro and Bliss

MONTHLY REVIEW PRESS, NEW YORK
monthlyreview.org

5 4 3 2 1

Contents

Preface

BY ANY IMAGINABLE DEFINITION of the working class, I was born into it. Almost every member of my extended family—parents, grandparents, uncles, aunts, and cousins—were wage laborers. They mined coal, hauled steel, made plate glass, labored on construction sites and as office secretaries, served the wealthy as domestic workers, clerked in company stores, cleaned offices and homes, took in laundry, cooked on tugboats, even unloaded trucks laden with dynamite. I joined the labor force at twelve and have been in it ever since, delivering newspapers, serving as a night watchman at a state park, doing clerical work in a factory, grading papers for a professor, selling life insurance, teaching in colleges and universities, arbitrating labor disputes, consulting for attorneys, desk clerking at a hotel, editing a magazine and books. I have spearheaded union organizing campaigns and helped in others. For more than thirty years, I taught workers in several labor studies programs, people in every imaginable occupation, from plumbers, bricklayers, postal employees, chemical workers, garment workers, and elevator operators to librarians, nurses, airline pilots, firefighters, and teachers. I once worked for the United Farm Workers Union, meeting campesinos and campesinas and helping them in legal disputes and collective bargaining.

As an academic my fields were labor economics and the relationship between capital and labor. I was most interested in *work*, especially how it is structured and controlled in capitalist economies. My growing understanding of this helped me to grasp the fundamental cleavage between working people and their bosses. Employees, I came to see, might win better wages, hours, and working conditions through organizing labor unions and agitating politically, under the umbrella of political organizations or parties. They have certainly achieved a great deal in nearly every country in the world using such means. Capitalism is a resilient system, however, and those who control its operations are relentless in their efforts both to prevent labor organizing and to beat back whatever gains unions and working-class political organizations have won. With rare exceptions, the power of capital has remained intact. Gains made have soon enough been taken back. Victorious revolutions have, in time, been reversed.

The conclusion I have reached is that fundamental, radical change, the kind implied in the title of this book, will not happen unless the working class and its allies attack capitalism and its multiple oppressions head-on, on every front, all the time. This is the presumption underlying this book. Struggles must be undertaken and coordinated against employers, the state, the mainstream media, those who run our schools, the police, the prison system, against racism, against patriarchy, against the destruction of the environment, against mega-church evangelicals, against the rise of fascism, against imperialism, and many other persons and institutions. Only such an all-out offensive has any chance of consigning capitalism to history's dustbin. Only this can give us hope of building a fundamentally new society, one with grassroots democracy, economic planning, a sustainable environment, meaningful work, and substantive equality in as many aspects of life as possible.

It would be impossible to list every person who has influenced what is said in this book. But let me single out John Bellamy Foster for tutoring me in matters concerning capital's catastrophic assault on our environment; Paul Le Blanc for his fine work in many of the areas discussed in this book; historian Michael Roberto for reading some of the chapters and making helpful suggestions; Henry Giroux for his encouragement and lifetime of work on critical education; the late David Houston for encouraging my budding radicalism; Herbert Chesler for teaching me so much about labor unions; and my comrades at Monthly Review Press, Martin Paddio and Susie Day. Karen Korenoski deserves special thanks for helping me understand the daily oppression of women and for being my partner through good times and bad. Finally, thanks, Erin Clermont, for your excellent copy editing.

To Lucia, Irene, Karen, Tara, and Tatiana,

the women who have held up more than half of my world.

1—The Working Class

In 2017, Daniel Fetonte was elected to the National Political Committee of the Democratic Socialists of America (DSA), a rapidly growing left-wing organization in the United States. Fetonte was co-chair of the Austin, Texas, branch of the DSA and had been involved in labor union organizing for many years. However, he had also been employed by the Combined Law Enforcement Associations of Texas, the largest police union in the state, with a membership of 21,000 police officers. When DSA members learned of this, many raised objections, arguing that anyone representing cops, who are the perpetrators of assaults, including numerous murders, on working people, especially if they are black, should not be an officer in an organization such as the DSA.[1]

TOWARD A DEFINITION OF THE WORKING CLASS

Fetonte has since resigned from the DSA, but the furor over his election to its board of directors raised a more general question, one it seems best to answer at the beginning of a book like this. What exactly is the working class? Is everyone who works for a wage a member of it? Perhaps in an abstract sense, this is so. But in terms of changing the world, this is a useless definition. Police and prison guards have labor unions. They are paid wages and take orders from supervisors. They are clearly workers. But they are not champions of the rights of other employees. Quite the contrary, as all of capitalist history shows. It would be even more preposterous to include principal corporate officials (including lawyers, accountants, and other highly paid shills and apologists for businesses), top political office holders, Wall Street's elites, and so forth. Those who occupy these positions may have salaries, but they are almost uniformly hostile to everything that might benefit those we normally think of as working class. They will never transform the world except in ways that keep themselves employed, powerful, and rich. To include the CEO of Goldman Sachs in the working class along with farm laborers makes a mockery of the very conception of a class that could create a new world.

By contrast, professional athletes, actors, and musicians, some of whom earn extremely high wages, at least in the United States and a few other countries, are potential allies of radical transformation. They often grew up poor and have sympathy for those who are oppressed, particularly people of color, as evidenced by their support for an end to police brutality in minority communities. In addition, not all of those in these occupations are rich, and they face insecurities like those of most workers. The labor of other relatively well-remunerated employees, such as doctors, engineers, and college professors, is also becoming more like those of most workers. Physicians are as likely today to work for hospitals as to be in private practice. Their jobs and those of other professionals are facing many of the modern forms of corporate control of the labor process—constant surveillance, de-skilling, mechanization—as most other workers have long endured.[2]

If we assume that a necessary condition to be included in the working class is wage labor, we will miss hundreds of millions who are not paid wages but labor in such a way that capital benefits. Many businesses, often with the participation of colleges and universities, take on unpaid interns. Schools promote this as a reason for students to attend their institutions. They claim that interns will get invaluable experience, opening doors for full-time employment. Businesses, on the other hand, get free publicity along with free labor. To the extent that interns do work normally done by wage laborers, they benefit the employer in the same way as paid workers do.[3]

A much larger group consists of everyone who works full-time doing unpaid reproductive labor, efforts that are critical for the production of the labor force. Largely comprising women, this group's work includes not only bearing children but all aspects of childcare, food shopping and preparation, nurturing, family gatherings and vacations, preparation for schooling, chauffeuring, and many other tasks. All this effort greatly profits employers, because they get young people trained in skills companies need but do not have to pay for, such as obedience, literacy, decent health, competitiveness. To exclude the millions who do these things full-time from the working class would be to exclude an enormous number of people with grievances severe enough that they might want to radically transform the world.

Unemployment is a fact of life in capitalist economies, which generate an enormous reserve of unutilized labor. Most members of this pool are without means, and desperate for work and money. It is almost always the case that racial minorities are overrepresented among the unemployed. Given that the unemployed are potential wage laborers, they are part of the working class. There are also millions worldwide who are not in the labor force, which is defined as the employed plus the unemployed. In the rich capitalist countries, discouraged workers, those who had given up looking for work because of limited job availability, rose greatly during the severe financial crisis of the last decade. There are others whose attachment to the labor market is sporadic but who would like a job. As with the unemployed, most of these must be considered in the working class.

Noted economist Samir Amin states that there are three billion peasants in the world today. The peasant rights organization La Via Campesina says that half of the world's people are peasants.[4] These are small farmers living in the world's countrysides. We will see in chapter 3 how the lands of feudal serfs were expropriated to help give birth to capitalism and how such land thefts, backed by state and corporate threats, violence, and dubious legal rulings, have continued to the present day, throughout the world. This has thrown peasants off their land and into despair and rebellion. Small farmers have been committing suicide in many countries, even in rich nations. An estimated forty-seven farmers in India commit suicide every day, crushed by debts, bad weather, falling prices for crops, and the rapaciousness of global capitalists, who buy or otherwise seize large parcels of land and utilize agribusiness techniques to lower costs and undermine the capacity of peasants to compete.[5] But peasants are not just ending their lives, they are also rebelling. Again using India as an example, rebellions, led by guerillas inspired by the writings and actions of the Chinese revolutionary Mao Zedong, have engaged in long-term military actions and land takeovers.[6] Mao's inspiration is appropriate, given that he led a successful revolution as the head of a peasant army.[7]

There has been considerable debate as to whether peasants are workers.[8] They are, for the most part, small farmers and hence not wage earners. Strictly speaking, then, they are not employees. However, given their exploitation at the hands of landlords, their often appalling treatment by the state, and their willingness to revolt, they are potential allies of the working class. And they often engage in some wage labor to make ends meet. Their children take jobs in the cities and send money home. Peasants are typically not far removed from the working class. Their struggles should be universally supported by working people. The worker-peasant alliance Mao Zedong worked to establish in China is a worthy goal today.[9]

The expropriation of peasant lands pushes farmers into the cities of the world. When the Industrial Revolution was advancing across Europe, landless peasants migrated in large numbers to the United States. There, they were absorbed by the new, giant factories owned by the nation's biggest capitalists, such as United States Steel and Ford Motor Company. Now, however, they cannot all become hands for businesses to exploit directly, because the machine intensity of modern production means relatively lower labor usage. The mechanization utilized in the rich capitalist nations is now used by capitalists in the poor countries. China is a critical center of manufacturing production, with employment of more than 100 million. There are signs that the growth of this workforce is slowing a bit, the result of modern corporate efficiency techniques, including mechanization. As this inevitably happens, China's reserve labor army will grow, and it will be difficult to absorb its members in formal types of employment.[10]

What happens to redundant peasants? They become members of the reserve army and must eke out a living as best they can. In every large city in the world, but especially in the Global South— (a term to describe those countries with relatively low per capita incomes; most are former colonies of the rich nations)—there are rings of slums, teeming with jobless and propertyless people.[11] A common way to earn a living in such places is to sell something in what are called "informal markets." Scholar Martha Allen Chen, an expert on the informal economy, describes some of the types of labor in the informal sectors of the global economy:

> Street vendors in Mexico City; push-cart vendors in New York City; rickshaw pullers in Calcutta; jitney drivers in Manila; garbage collectors in Bogotá; and roadside barbers in Durban. Those who work on the streets or in the open air are the most visible informal workers. Other informal workers are engaged in small shops and workshops that repair bicycles and motorcycles; recycle scrap metal; make furniture and metal parts; tan leather and stitch shoes; weave, dye, and print cloth; polish diamonds and other gems; make and embroider garments; sort and sell cloth, paper, and metal waste; and more. The least visible informal workers, the majority of them women, work from their homes. Home-based workers are to be found around the world. They include garment workers in Toronto; embroiderers on the island of Madeira; shoemakers in Madrid; and assemblers of electronic parts in Leeds. Other categories of work that tend to be informal in both developed and developing countries include: casual workers in restaurants and hotels; subcontracted janitors and security guards; day laborers in construction and

agriculture; piece-rate workers in sweatshops; and temporary office helpers or off-site data processors.[12]

Hundreds of millions of men, women, and children are doing these kinds of work.

In the rich nations, many of those laboring in the informal economy would be called independent contractors. But in the Global South, to call what those who scavenge garbage dumps in the Philippines for salable items either "independent" or "contractors" is a cruel joke. The same could be said, however, of many taxicab, limousine, FedEx, Uber, and Lyft drivers in the United States. Not to mention those who sell items on eBay and Craigslist. For the first group, a legal fiction is used that allows companies to claim that the workers are not employees because they must lease the vehicles from them and pay expenses. It is ironic that 18,000 New York City cabbies have joined the New York Taxi Workers Alliance (NYTWA) to fight for better pay, conditions, and benefits.[13] This hardly sounds like a group of independent businesspersons. In addition, they are carefully monitored electronically while driving by their de facto employers.

With most of the categories surveyed here, it has become typical for people to be in more than one of them, either at the same or different times. A woman may be a homemaker and a wage laborer; in fact, this is increasingly common. There are tens of millions in the world who are involuntary part-time workers, meaning that they are partly employed and unemployed. Those who are not in the labor force, and thus neither employed nor unemployed, might seek jobs when economic conditions improve. The two to three billion peasants worldwide often, as noted above, do wage labor at some time during the year. The same goes for the hundreds of millions of informal-sector workers, who may also work for wages when jobs are available. For example, if street sellers of trinkets in Mexico City are offered short-term employment cleaning churches, then they are both working on their own as a seller and for someone else as a cleaner. At one time, I did several types of work during the same period. I was a full-time college teacher, an independent contractor, and a part-time teacher. Such disparate work locations can generate conflicting feelings about one's class position and the potential for solidarity with others.

Situating the Working Class Quantitatively and Qualitatively

Quantity. Labor expert Ursula Huws has given us an interesting breakdown of work (not workers, but what they do).[14] She devised a table that shows four categories of activity. She distinguishes between labor that benefits capitalists as a whole and work that enriches particular employers. The first helps to reproduce capitalist relations of production, while the second produces profits. Then she counterposes effort that is remunerated and that which is not. We then have 1) paid and unpaid work that reproduces the labor-capital relationship; and 2) paid and unpaid work that increases the profits of individual businesses. The four cells in the Table 1 (below) are labeled A, B, C, and D.

The examples in the table's cells should be self-explanatory; further elaboration is in chapter 2. Readers will no doubt be able to think of many other illustrations. Huws discusses several complicated conundrums with respect to her tabular breakdown, and these need not concern us here. What is important is that cell C now contains the lion's share of the world's labor. As governments everywhere, in alliance with corporate capital, have privatized more and more public services, work in cell A has shifted to C.

TABLE 1.	PAID	UNPAID
Reproduction (help all businesses)	(A) e.g., public school teachers	(B) e.g., homemakers
Profits (help one business)	(C) e.g., autoworker, sales clerk	(D) e.g., groceries self-checkout

For example, trash services, school bus drivers, operations of toll highways, and many other state-financed services have been turned over to private, profit-seeking businesses. Similarly, much unpaid work has now been commodified, such as childcare and food preparation, shifting labor from B to C.

What is critical about this is that as more work is done under the necessary condition that capitalists make money, the power of workers is increased, as will be explained in chapter 2. The capacity of those who labor for wages to shut down production represents a tremendous potential power, which could be harnessed to help change the world.

If we move from work to workers, what can we say quantitatively about the working class? The International Labor Organization (ILO), an agency of the United Nations, publishes a yearly summary of labor-related data called the World Employment Social Outlook (WESO).[15] For 2018, the ILO estimates a global labor force of just under 3.5 billion, out of a population of 7.6 billion. The labor force includes all those who are employed and unemployed, excluding those below fifteen years of age (although the age minimum varies somewhat by country and some nations have upper age limits). The 2018 estimate for unemployment, which only includes those not employed but seeking and available for work, is 194 million. This means that there will be about 3.3 billion employed persons. Of the employed, some 1.8 billion are estimated to be employees, that is, wage and salary earners, which is 51.4 percent of the world's labor force. This can be considered a lower limit of the global working class, although some within this group are closely allied to capital or are capitalists themselves.

To the employed wage and salary earners, we must add those in the reserve army of labor. Sociologist Jamil Jonna calculated, using ILO data for 2011, that if we add the unemployed, what the ILO terms the "vulnerably employed," and those not in the labor force for whatever reason, we get a reserve army that is more than 70 percent larger than the number of wage and salary workers.[16] Here is a description of "vulnerable employment":

People in vulnerable employment are the self-employed . . . and unpaid but working family members in the household of the self-employed. In most of the world, vulnerable employment is what is known as casual work; the workers who do this do not have formal arrangements with an employer, such as a labor contract with stipulated wages. A man selling lottery tickets on a street corner, a woman hawking tamales in a parking lot, or a teenager offering rickshaw rides are examples of vulnerable employment. A child helping her mother sell the tamales is an example of an unpaid family member doing vulnerable work.[17]

The ILO predicts vulnerable employment to be 1.4 billion in 2018. Some of these, especially in the rich countries, are prosperous independent contractors, but most are not. And hundreds of millions must be counted as part of the reserve army of labor.

The 2018 estimate for persons not in the labor force is 2.2 billion. Some are incapable of working, but others have given up seeking employment, labor as homemakers, or are unpaid family members doing vulnerable work. It is not possible to discover the overlap between the vulnerably employed and those not in the labor force. Suffice it to say that, counting the officially unemployed, there must be more than a billion people to add to the working class.

To these we can add most of those languishing in prisons, especially in the pack of countries that lead in incarcerations, namely the United States, China, Russia, and Brazil. These hold about one-half of the 11 million persons locked up worldwide. Given that most of the nations in the world do not imprison people at anywhere near the rate of these four countries, it is reasonable to suggest that those confined in their cells could work. Of course, they do work while in jail, but under involuntary conditions, a modern form of slavery.[18]

The ILO's age cutoff for data on the international labor force is fifteen. Yet, even in wealthy states, children younger than this engage in wage labor. In poor places, child labor is much more common. Most child workers are in agriculture, live in peasant households, and many are unpaid family members in the informal economy. The latter group has already been accounted for in the numbers above. A rough estimate of children in the labor force, which assumes that they are concentrated in industry and services, in the same proportion as that between those less than fifteen years of age and total child labor, yields about 33 million child wage laborers.[19]

We have made no account yet of peasants, many of whom have grievances against global capitalism and could be important allies of the working class. There are some 500 million peasant farms in the world, and if we assume just four family members per farm, we have two billion peasants, including children.[20] However, many peasants do wage work to supplement whatever income they earn by selling crops. In China, the state-sponsored destruction of collective farms and their replacement by small individual plots of land has forced peasants to seek wage work in urban industrial areas. Then, when industrial production falls for any reason (economic downturn, for example), they are forced to return to their rural villages. This means that the number of peasants can fluctuate enormously. Thus, it is not possible to know exactly how many peasants there are, though they almost certainly number more than one billion.[21]

The purpose of this foray into statistics is not to specify with some exactness how large the working class is. Rather, it is to demonstrate that, at any given time, there are several billion people working, in the reserve army of labor, or peasants. Should ways be found to organize and unify, say, even 20 percent of them, they could surely change the world.

Refining the Numbers

Not only is the working class, broadly construed, large in number, it is also diverse. A basic difference is between male and female. Today there are nearly 1.4 billion women in the labor force, 39 percent of the total.[22] This fraction is considerably less than it is in the nations of the Global North (the wealthy capitalist countries).

It is 47 percent in the United States, which is close to the percentages for most rich capitalist nations.[23] The global percentage will rise as capital extends its geographical penetration, and as women continue to demand access to paid employment.

Women wage earners are still concentrated in the service sector (with nearly 1.7 billion service workers in the world),[24] where wages are lower than in industry and the professions. They earn less than men even in the same or similar jobs. A recent United Nations study found that "once in the paid labor force, women everywhere find themselves earning less than men for the same types of work; engaging more frequently in unskilled, low-wage labor; or spending less time in income-generating work and more time in unpaid caregiving work at home."[25] Women are also less likely to be literate than men, do more reproductive labor than men, whether in the labor force or not, are less likely than men to have access to health care, suffer many more sexual assaults in their homes and workplaces, more often than not lack maternity leave, and are discouraged in school from studying mathematics and science.[26]

Although gender represents the most basic split in the working class and perhaps, given the long history of patriarchy, the most important, the laboring masses are divided in many other ways. They are fragmented by race, ethnicity, nationality, religion, and language. A brief look at some data from the United States shows the remarkable disparities between black and white members of the working class.[27] Median black family income is barely 60 percent that of whites, a little more than ten percentage points higher than it was in 1949. Black median household net worth is just 5 percent that of whites. Blacks earn less than whites at all levels of education. Astonishingly, "a $10,000 increase in the average annual wage of an occupation is associated with a seven-percentage-point decrease in the proportion of black men in that occupation."[28] Besides earnings, when we consider poverty, unemployment, health, education, housing, life expectancy, infant mortality, or the criminal justice system, we must conclude that "having a black skin, in and of itself, is a grave economic and social disadvantage, while having a white skin confers considerable advantage."[29] We would find similar differences in many parts of the world, and find much the same if we examine the data from South Africa, where those with black skins are a majority.[30]

There are numerous ethnic groups in the world, and there are clear differences in terms of how ethnic groups fare. Han Chinese discriminate against Uighurs. Indigenous people everywhere are treated as second-class citizens, unworthy of the dignity others expect as a matter of course. Kurds face mistreatment from Arabs and Iranians. The same can be said for nationality. Palestinians suffer horrible abuse at the hands of Israelis. Turkish guest workers are mistreated by Germans. Haitians are urged and sometimes compelled to leave the Dominican Republic. Mexican immigrants in the United States often toil as farm laborers for subsistence wages, and Donald Trump accuses them of being rapists and murderers. Religious discrimination is also common globally. Trump routinely says or implies that Muslims are terrorists. All these forms of bigotry, often built into a nation's institutional structure, translate into inferior economic and social outcomes for those who must endure them.[31]

The categories that mark the diversity of the working class always intersect. That is, a woman will have a nationality, perhaps an ethnicity, a religion, a race. Such intersections can compound or reduce the impact of discrimination. For example, a black woman in the United States faces the slings and arrows of both racism and patriarchy, whereas a black man confronts racism but not patriarchy. This doesn't mean, of course, that patriarchy is not in some ways detrimental to men, because it is. But it is not the same for men and women. The importance of these intersections, and in fact of each intersecting category taken separately, is that, though all workers have much in common, their differences are important too, in terms of the likelihood of the working class changing the world.

Working people obtain most of their incomes by selling their labor power to employers. However, wages vary enormously both within and among countries. In the United States 2.2 million employees in 2016 were paid at or below the federal minimum wage of $7.25 per hour, which for a 2,000-hour work year was equal to or less than $14,500.[32] In that year, there were athletes, popular singers, and actors whose annual wages exceeded five million dollars. And just as overall incomes have become steadily more unequal, so too have wages, not just in the United States but in many other nations.[33] Those at the bottom are falling further behind those at the top, which raises an interesting question: What do workers earning the minimum wage have in common with those at the top of the wage structure, other than that they are wage laborers and members of the working class? Their life experiences are worlds apart. If we compare wages internationally, the disparities are more glaring. Average monthly wages in Pakistan are about 8 percent of those in the United States. What are the similarities of an average Pakistani wage earner and an average earner in the United States?[34] It is difficult to think of many.

We need not compare the lowest and the highest wage recipients to intuit that workers with different incomes might not share worldviews or have the same class consciousness. There is an enormous global middle class, roughly those households whose incomes (most, but not all, of which are wages) lie between the 30th and 70th percentiles of the income distribution. Economist and expert on global inequality Branco Milanovic has shown that there are about 380 million people in this group from China, India, Indonesia, Brazil, and Egypt alone.[35] As incomes in this segment of the world's working classes have risen, it may be that many within it might rationally believe they have a stake in the political and economic status quo. They might not have much commitment to changing the world.

QUALITY

Although the quality of work and of life varies tremendously within the working class, there is a good deal of misery in both. However, if the world is to be changed, those of us whose circumstances are well above the global average and far superior to those who live at the edge of subsistence have a stake in the liberation of what psychiatrist Franz Fanon called "the wretched of the earth."[36] If they are not free, how can any of us be? As the socialist leader Eugene V. Debs said in 1918 to the U.S. court that was about to sentence him to prison for violating the Sedition Act, "Your Honor, years ago I recognized my kinship with all living beings, and I made up my mind that I was not one bit better than the meanest on earth. I said then, and I say now, that while there is a lower class, I am in it, and while there is a criminal element I am of it, and while there is a soul in prison, I am not free."[37]

Let us look at child labor. The ILO estimates that of the 151.6 million child laborers (the ILO's age range is five to seventeen years), 72.5 million toil in hazardous work. The ILO says this about such hazards:

> In general, hazardous work may include night work and long hours of work, exposure to physical, psychological, or sexual abuse; work underground, under water, at dangerous heights or in confined spaces; work with dangerous machinery, equipment, and tools, or which involves the manual handling or transport of heavy loads; and work in an unhealthy environment which may, for example, expose children to hazardous substances, agents, or processes, or to temperatures, noise levels, or vibrations damaging their health.[38]

The number of juveniles in hazardous work includes what the ILO terms "the worst forms of child labor," which include slavery, prostitution, and drug trafficking. However, because data on these abominations are difficult to find, there is no doubt that there are more child workers than the ILO estimates indicate. In Bombay alone, there are thousands of child sex workers:

> When Mira, a sweet-faced virgin with golden brown skin, refused to have sex, she was dragged into a torture chamber in a dark alley used for "breaking in" new girls. She was locked in a

narrow, windowless room without food or water. On the fourth day, when she had still refused to work, one of the madam's thugs, called a goonda, wrestled her to the floor and banged her head against the concrete until she passed out. When she awoke, she was naked; a rattan cane smeared with pureed red chili peppers had been shoved up her vagina. Later, she was raped by the goonda. "They torture you until you say yes," Mira recently recounted during an interview here. "Nobody hears your cries."[39]

Here is an example of work that is merely "hazardous," as told by Irfana, a Pakistani girl sold to a brick kiln owner:

My master bought, sold, and traded us like livestock, and sometimes he shipped us great distances. The boys were beaten frequently to make them work long hours. The girls were often violated. My best friend got ill after she was raped, and when she couldn't work, the master sold her to a friend of his in a village a thousand kilometers away. Her family was never told where she was sent, and they never saw her again.[40]

Multiple types of adult work are extremely dangerous and detrimental to health. There are six million construction workers in the United States, and construction has the highest rate of occupational fatalities. Asbestos has been killing workers for many years. More than one million construction workers are at risk from asbestos, which causes crippling and then fatal lung disease.[41] Worldwide, there are 180 million construction workers. Most work in the informal economy, where health risks are greatest. In India, 30 percent of construction workers are women, almost all of whom are informally employed.[42] Labor writer and photographer David Bacon tells about an asbestos worker in Los Angeles:

Sergio Ruiz Nuñez is a lonely man.
    Remembering his wife and daughter left behind in Mexico City a year ago, his chest starts to heave. He cannot speak. To

hide the water welling up in the corners of his eyes, he turns away.

Ruiz is a big man, with muscles built by heavy labor bulking up under his tee-shirt. But as his feelings overcome him, his size makes him seem vulnerable.

"You know," he finally says when he can speak again, "when you come to this country you have so many illusions. There are so many things you think you'll do, and you have all the will in the world to get ahead and help your family. You put your soul into your work, your heart and your life.

"And then you find the reality, and you leave those illusions and romantic ideas behind."

Every weekday morning, and most Saturdays, Ruiz gets up and hauls himself to the job, another old building undergoing renovation. There he puts on a white paper-like suit, complete with hood and booties like a kid's pajamas. Sometimes he has to put on two of them. Then he dons a mask, and often a breathing apparatus. He walks into a special area of the building, sectioned off with an airtight seal of tape and plastic sheets.

And he starts to strip asbestos, possibly the most dangerous building material ever used.[43]

There are between 60 and 75 million garment workers globally, most of them women, many laboring out of their homes, very poorly paid, producing our clothing and footwear in often dangerous conditions. Subcontracted workers in Bangkok earn as little as nine dollars a day for nine hours of labor.[44] Political economist John Smith describes the horrific collapse of a plaza housing textile factories in Bangladesh:

The collapse of Rana Plaza, an eight-story building housing several textile factories, a bank, and some shops in an industrial district north of Dhaka, Bangladesh's capital, on 24 April 2013, killing 1,133 garment workers and wounding 2,500, was one of the worst workplace disasters in recorded history. This

disaster, and garment workers' grief, rage, and demands for justice, stirred feelings of sympathy and solidarity from working
people around the world—and a frantic damage-limitation exercise by the giant corporations that rely on Bangladeshi factories
for their products yet deny any responsibility for the atrocious
wages, living, and working conditions of those who produce all
their stuff. Adding to the sense of outrage felt by many is the
fact that, the day before, cracks had opened up in the building's
structure and an initial inspection resulted in its evacuation and
a recommendation that it remain closed. Next morning a bank
and shops on the ground floor obeyed this advice, but thousands of garment workers were ordered back to work on pain
of dismissal. When generators illegally installed on the top floor
were started up the building collapsed. Jyrki Raina, general sec-
retary of IndustriALL, an international union federation, called
it "mass industrial slaughter."[45]

In 2010, workers at the Foxconn plant in Longhua Subdistrict,
Shenzhen, China, began committing suicide. So many killed
themselves that the company installed safety nets to catch those
trying to jump to their deaths. Foxconn is a major assembler of the
Apple iPhone. It employs 1.3 million employees worldwide—only
Walmart and McDonald's have more. There are some 18 million
electronics workers globally. The work is stressful, tedious, and
mind- and body-numbing. Employers use all the labor-process
control techniques now available, including electronic monitoring. Neurological and respiratory diseases are common, as are
cancers. Many workers are women.[46]

In an extract from his book, *The One Device: The Secret History
of the iPhone*, Brian Merchant offers a description of life in the
Foxconn suicide mill:

"It's not a good place for human beings," says one of the young
men, who goes by the name Xu. He'd worked in Longhua for
about a year, until a couple of months ago, and he says the

conditions inside are as bad as ever. "There is no improvement since the media coverage," Xu says. The work is very high pressure and he and his colleagues regularly logged 12-hour shifts. Management is both aggressive and duplicitous, publicly scolding workers for being too slow and making them promises they don't keep, he says. His friend, who worked at the factory for two years and chooses to stay anonymous, says he was promised double pay for overtime hours but got only regular pay. They paint a bleak picture of a high-pressure working environment where exploitation is routine and where depression and suicide have become normalised.

"It wouldn't be Foxconn without people dying," Xu says. "Every year people kill themselves. They take it as a normal thing."[47]

When I was a teacher I showed a film about women from the countryside in the Philippines who came to Manila, some seeking more personal freedom and others hoping to send money back to their families. Those that found employment in electronics burned out by their late twenties, when they were discarded and replaced by younger women. One employer said, in discussing the work, "These women can take a lot of abuse."

In the rich capitalist countries, not many work in agriculture. In the poorer nations, farm labor has been falling, but there are still 866 million men, women, and children planting, tending, and harvesting our crops.[48] Their living and laboring conditions are, in general, abysmal.

The grocery stores of the United States are filled with produce grown in Mexico. David Bacon describes what farmworkers face there:

In the fields, a single portable bathroom might serve a whole crew of several hundred, with a metal drum on wheels providing the drinking water. . . . Toddlers wander among the seated workers, some of them nursing on baby bottles and others, their faces smeared with dirt, chewing on the onions. A few sleep in the rows, or in little makeshift beds of blankets in the vegetable bins. . . . As the morning sun illuminates the faces of the workers, it reveals dozens of young girls and boys. By rough count, perhaps a quarter of the workers here are anywhere from 6 or 7 years old to 15 or 16. . . . Honorina Ruiz is 6. She sits in front of a pile of green onions. . . . She lines up eight or nine onions, straightening out their roots and tails. Then she knocks the dirt off, puts a rubber band around them and adds the bunch to those already in the box beside her. She's too shy to say more than her name, but she seems proud to be able to do what her brother Rigoberto, at 13, is very good at. . . . These are Mexico's forgotten children.[49]

The hard life of the Joad family in John Steinbeck's *The Grapes of Wrath* is reality for hundreds of millions of farmworkers today, everywhere they toil the fields.

It is difficult to determine how many people are employed in transportation, warehousing, and logistics globally. In the United States, there are 5.4 million workers in the first two categories.[50] There may be nearly six million truck drivers in the world. It would surely be no exaggeration to suggest that there are tens of millions of workers in transportation, warehousing, and logistics hubs that have been built in and near major cities around the world. In the United States, around Chicago, a major center for all modes of transport, are employed "some 200,000 workers in the top five warehouse occupations in about 200 to 300 warehouses, as well as 39,410 heavy tractor-trailer truck drivers, 23,990 light truck and delivery drivers, and 17,550 industrial truck and tractor operators, to mention a few other occupations."[51] Similar employment clusters exist in the Los Angeles, New York–New Jersey, and Memphis metropolitan areas. Internationally, wherever goods are shipped, flown, or trucked in in large volume, there are tens of thousands of people transporting products, loading and unloading them, and directing the complex traffic and output flows.

Again, using the United States as an example, the main attraction of these hubs is a ready supply of cheap black and immigrant labor. Chicago has a high poverty rate, and black unemployment rates are much higher than the national average. The expropriation of peasant lands and the impact of cheap U.S. imports have sent millions of immigrants to the United States, mainly to cities like Chicago:

> A 2010 survey of warehouse workers in Will County in the heart of the Chicago metro area conducted by Warehouse Workers for Justice found that 48 percent of warehouse workers were African American, 38 percent Latino, 11 percent white non-Latino, and the rest a mixture of Asians, Arabs, Native Americans, and "others." Women compose about a quarter of the warehouse workforce. In addition, there are truck, rail, and communications workers in large numbers passing through this massive agglomeration of capital and labor. For the thousands of warehouse workers, wages are low and employment insecure. The pay of the major warehouse occupations in Will County ranged from $9.28 an hour to $14.55 in 2010, almost two-thirds are paid below the poverty level, and all are below the government's low-wage level. As a result, 37 percent hold second jobs and 25 percent rely on government benefits of one sort or another. Some 63 percent are employed by temporary agencies rather than by warehouse outfits, third-party logistics (3PL) firms, or retail giants such as Wal-Mart that own or use the warehouses, and receive little in the way of benefits.[52]

We hear a great deal about the need for highly skilled technical workers and the concomitant need for future employees to obtain more schooling, especially in engineering, science, and mathematics. Yet hundreds of millions work in occupations that do not require such skills or education. If you were asked how many people in the United States are automobile workers; secretaries, administrative assistants, and office support personnel; clerks; restaurant workers; security employees; custodians; and medical workers, the chances are good that you would understate the numbers. In 2015, there were 63 million in these jobs, out of a total national employment of a little over 140 million. That is 45 percent. And for each of these, it would be easy to construct a litany of woes: the carpal tunnel of auto workers and clerks, the burns on the hands and arms of cooks, the aching legs and feet of every worker who is required to stand for long periods of time, the stress of medical workers, the constant watchfulness of the boss, the insecurities and fears, the absence of hope. And this is in the richest country in the world. Consider how much more is borne by those in the world's poorest places. I wrote an essay a few years ago titled "Work Is Hell."[53] For most, indeed it is. As for the future, the U.S. Bureau of Labor Statistics tells us that the occupations that will have the most job growth between 2016 and 2026 are, for the most part, those that do not require advanced education or sophisticated technical skills. Of the top twenty-one, we can say this about at least fifteen.[54] Personal care aides top the list. Is there any reason to believe the facts are different in the rest of the world?

Reproductive labor, central to the production of labor power, is overwhelmingly the province of women. Cooking, cleaning, nursing babies, raising children, with all that it implies—endless food and clothing shopping, the hassles of schooling, and multiple other tasks, nonstop, on-call twenty-four hours every day. In the Global South, clothes must be made by hand and food grown in family plots. Washing garments is done the old-fashioned way, by hand, often in a stream or river. The skills needed to do all these chores are considerable: dexterity, the ability to plan and multitask, nursing and counseling capacities. Yet "their work is so devalued that an estimate of its value is not included in the Gross Domestic Product. The unpaid labor of poor single women with children is considered so worthless that they have been forced to give it up and seek wage labor, often taking care of the children of others while their own kids are attended haphazardly or not at all."[55] Circumstances in India for homemakers, reflecting the conditions of women in that country, have gotten so bad that more than 20,000 have committed suicide annually since 1997, the first year such a number could be calculated.[56]

The woes of the unemployed, those in prison, those who have become too discouraged to seek work, those in vulnerable employment, and peasants always threatened with loss of their land, can easily be imagined. Or the despair that drives the unemployed and the discouraged to drugs and alcohol, often leading to hypertension, heart attack, cirrhosis of the liver, mental illness, and suicide. The rage of those incarcerated, especially those unjustly accused and those too poor or powerless to have had any hope for justice. The desperation of those compelled to survive by combing the mountains of tin waste in Bolivia for scraps of the metal. The fear of peasants that their land will be stolen by thugs in the pay of the large corporations or their own governments. Or the oppression of those small landowners who are bombed mercilessly—in Syria, Yemen, Iraq, Afghanistan today, Vietnam and East Timor yesterday—for seeking to free their country from the grip of colonial or imperial rapaciousness.

There are good jobs in the world. Readers may have one, and most will at least know those who do. But on the whole, the working class labors under harsh conditions, with precariousness the norm. And as we shall soon see, all so that a relatively small number of individuals can be rich and powerful.

2—Some Theoretical Considerations

To answer a question in any field of inquiry, we need a theoretical framework. This requires us to set basic assumptions, trace out the logic of these suppositions, and then test this logic against what has happened in the world of experience. If we assume, for example, that businesses single-mindedly seek to maximize their profits, then the logic of this would lead us to predict that employers will oppose an increase in the minimum wage because this would reduce profits. It would also lead us to predict that a higher minimum wage would reduce employment, because as this wage rises, at least some employees will add more to corporate costs than to revenues, meaning that if employment does not fall, profits would, violating our assumption. We could then test to see if employers have indeed been hostile to minimum wage increases and if a higher minimum wage has in fact led to lower employment.

This chapter lays out an analytical scaffolding that will show that working people are exploited and expropriated, making it impossible for them to achieve real freedom, autonomy, and unalienated lives in a capitalist society. Thus, there are grounds for them to rebel to accomplish these things. (Whether and how is taken up in later chapters.) Throughout, remember that peasants are included as part of the working class, although sometimes they are examined separately from wage workers. Also, unless otherwise stated, the words employer, corporation, business, firm, capitalist, and capital are used interchangeably. The same is true for worker, employer, laborer, toiler, hand, and labor. The name Global North is used frequently as shorthand for the world's few rich capitalist countries: United States, Canada, Great Britain, the Scandinavian nations, France, Germany, Italy, the remainder of the countries in what used to be called Western Europe, Japan, Australia, and New Zealand. Global South encompasses the rest of the world, although there are a few nations that have made strides toward becoming members of the Global North, such as South Korea.

What Is Capitalism?

Capitalism is a social system built upon exploitation and expropriation. It is both an economy and a society, composed of multiple, connected elements. First, its central economic feature is production for the market, as opposed to production for use. It does not matter that people might need a product; if there is no market for it, it will not be produced. Putting this matter concretely, it means that those who control production are motivated by profits; if they do not expect to make money, they will not send goods and services to market. Second, the non-human means of production—land, machinery, tools, equipment, buildings, raw materials, and the like— are the private property of capitalists, who always comprise a small fraction of the population. Today, capital is organized in large global corporations, each controlling enormous amounts of productive property and cash resources.

Third, most people must sell their labor power, their capacity to work, to the owners of the means of production. Therefore, capitalist economies have labor markets, in which labor power is bought and sold. Those who sell this are free, but in a double sense. They are not bound personally to a superior, as were feudal serfs and slaves. However, they are also "free" of any significant means of production and are therefore compelled to find a buyer for their ability to work. They are not compelled to labor for a particular employer, but they must toil for some person, company, or entity. Failure to do so can have disastrous results, including death. Note that historically, as discussed in chapter 3, unfree labor, mostly slave, was critical to the birth and advance of capitalism. Unfortunately, slave labor is still utilized by capital.[1]

These economic characteristics of capitalism can be easily shown. The corporate pursuit of profits is too well known to require proof. Suffice it to mention that the Ford Motor Company knew that its Pinto model's fuel system would be prone to rupture if the car was struck from behind, possibly causing riders to burn to death. Yet its accountants estimated that it would be cheaper to let people die and perhaps pay a cash settlement than to reengineer the car.[2]

Consider wealth, which is the money value of everything that a person, a family, or a household owns. The most important forms of wealth are the means of production, given that everyone in a society depends on them to survive. Possession of these, whether directly or as ownership claims such as shares of corporate stock, is remarkably unequally divided in every capitalist country in the world.[3] One startling statistic says it all: "The three wealthiest people in the United States—Bill Gates, Jeff Bezos, and Warren Buffett—now own more wealth than the entire bottom half of the American population, a total of 160 million people or 63 million households."[4]

If wealth, especially that in the means of production, is so unequally divided, then it must be the case that most of the world's people do not own any wealth, or not enough to matter. If this is so, then they have no choice but to sell their labor power. Thus, the third feature of capitalism, the ubiquity of wage labor, is self-evident.

Exploitation of Wage Labor

Let us look now at the production of goods and services. Marx used a letter scheme to illustrate what we call the accumulation of capital, by which we mean the drive by capital to expand itself, indefinitely. This is represented by $M-C-C'-M'$. M is money capital, the starting point of capitalist production. Businesses must have money, obtained one way or another, to begin production. Loans, stock sales, and savings are three possible sources of cash. The goal of the owner of money capital is to expand it, to accumulate, to make M', which also stands for money, as much larger than the original M as possible. How can this be accomplished? It might be possible to lend the M at interest and secure a profit. But if every capitalist did this, nothing would be produced, and sooner or later, both lender and borrower would starve. The same logic applies to buying goods at one price and selling them at a higher price, as merchants do. The world could not be organized like this; merchants would have to find an ever-increasing supply of goods to sell. Who would produce these?

In what manner, then, does the owner of M, operating as a capitalist, take one sum of money and convert it into a larger sum? Suppose we assume that everything the business buys or sells is bought or sold at its market price, what mainstream economists call its "equilibrium price," one at which there are neither shortages nor surpluses. No one has special information or market power to command either a lower or a higher price for anything. If for some reason a buyer pays a greater price, its loss is matched by the seller's gain. There is, therefore, no net gain or loss for the system as a whole.

To begin production of a commodity, say cloth, cars, frozen pizzas, or the services provided by a group of physicians, the owner of the money capital, M, must enter the marketplace and purchase a set of commodities, C, which have the form of means of production. These include land, buildings, office space, tools, machinery, raw materials, and labor power. Inputs other than labor power are called "constant capital" (K), some of which are long-lasting and termed "fixed capital," like buildings and machinery, and some of which must be regularly replaced, like the raw materials used in each cycle of production. The capacity of workers to labor is termed "variable capital" (V). Both K and V are purchased at their currently typical market prices.

Once the C has been secured, our capitalist leaves the realm of the market and moves to the workplace. Today, as when capitalism was young, the places where people work can take many forms: a factory, warehouse, cubicle, home, school, bank, or anywhere there is an internet connection. Here is where capital and labor come face-to-face, so to speak, either directly or electronically. Marx said that when the workers enter the workplace, all they can expect is a "hiding."

Marx's wording gives us a clue as to what transpires in the change from C to C'. The two parties, capital and labor, do not face each other as equals, but as superior to inferior. One owns the workplace; the other has no choice but to labor for capital, if not in this workplace then in another. Capital's dominance is the ultimate source of the exploitation workers suffer at the hands of their employers.

To show this, Marx argued that the money exchanged in the purchase and sale of commodities must be proportional to the amount of time expended in their production. Commodities have both use values and exchange values. Cars and cell phones are obviously useful, as are wool cloth and glass mirrors. Here, they have nothing in common except that they are useful, as are or were all objects consumed by people in every mode of production. In capitalism, however, commodities are also exchanged, that is, they are bought and sold in markets, with the goal of not only satisfying needs but also making money. Though commodities are uniquely useful, in terms of exchange they have this in common: given the constant capital, it requires a certain amount of labor time to get the product to market.

Competition among capitals tends toward a position in which, for any given commodity, the labor time embedded in it is "average," that is, it reflects the average prevailing technology, the average intensity of labor, and the average skill of the workforce. A business that does not meet these conditions, using, for example, an inferior technology, would have to use more labor time than its rivals, and charge a higher price. Sooner or later, this capital would be forced from the market. If one capitalist introduces a superior technology, this business will use less labor time and be able to undersell its competitors. Its profits will, accordingly, be higher. However, competition will force the other firms in the market to also utilize this technology, eliminating the originating company's advantage.

In other words, the prices of commodities must, over the long run, reflect the time put forth to make them under average conditions of production. The costs of production are labor-time costs. Time is, indeed, money. But as assumed above, each commodity sells at its equilibrium price, meaning that when two commodities have the same price, the labor times in them must also be equal. Under the surface of the marketplace's money transactions is an exchange of labor times.

If the money we pay for a product is the equivalent of the time it takes to make it, how is it possible that profits can be extracted from the process of production? If in the purchase of K and V (together these equal the C in our letter scheme), and if in the sale of the final product (the C′), no profit can be made, where do profits originate?

Given that commodities tend to sell at a price equivalent, in money terms, to the cost of producing them, is there some commodity that can increase the value (the labor time) of a product? It cannot be the constant capital, because this is the result of labor expended in the past—"dead" labor, as Marx called it. The constant capital is inanimate, and all that happens when workers use it is that the labor time embedded in it is transferred to a new commodity, hour for hour. Nothing can be added by something that is not alive. The labor power, on the other hand, is "living" labor, elastic in a way that machinery, buildings, land, and tools are not.

To see what happens in the workplace, in the transition from C to C′, we need to know the cost of the labor power, reflected in the market as the wages of the employees.

Unlike other commodities, our capacity to work is not produced like loaves of bread or tee-shirts. Yet, it must come into being, like any other article that is bought and sold. For us to labor, for an average workday, week, year, lifetime, we must be fed, housed, clothed, nurtured, taught. The food we eat and the clothes we wear are the result of the expenditure of a certain amount of labor power. This necessary consumption must have within it a definite amount of labor time. If it is true that equal labor times are exchanged in the market, then we can say that the wage paid must be sufficient to purchase the subsistence bundle of commodities. It is true that employees might be paid less than this, and often are, but businesses cannot pay less than a survival wage indefinitely or their hired hands will either face deteriorating health or die.

Suppose that the daily subsistence basket of goods and services requires the use of five hours of average labor time. In terms of time, then, the wage must be at least equal to five hours. That is, the wage, when paid, must be the equivalent of the five hours of goods and services needed for survival. It must be enough to purchase the subsistence basket of goods and services. Let us further assume that the amount of constant capital used per day has two hours of labor time in it. This means that two hours of every worker's day must be devoted to paying for the machinery, tools, land, raw materials, and buildings used up every day. Note that the fixed capital, such as the machinery, is consumed bit by bit, depreciated each period until it wears out and must be replaced. Raw materials, on the other hand, are used up completely each day.

The total time costs are now seven hours, any seven hours, given that we assume the laborers work with an average level of intensity during each hour. For the business to break even, the day must be seven hours. This would allow for production of an output, which, when sold, would pay for the constant and variable capital used in production. It would also allow workers to buy the subsistence basket of goods and services.

Capitalist enterprise would not exist if every entity broke even. Profits are necessary. What is the source of these? One of the entitlements arising from ownership is to set the length of the working day. In one of the most powerful chapters in *Capital*, volume 1, titled "The Working Day," Marx shows that capital will make the working day as long as humanly possible, extending it whenever it can.[5] Men, women, and children in Marx's time routinely sweated twelve to eighteen hours a day.

If, for example, the average working day is twelve hours, and the average constant and variable costs are seven hours, as they are for our representative firm, then there are five hours that cost the employer nothing. These hours are "surplus" labor time. Yet, during these hours, workers are expected to put forth an average amount of effort. So, they produce the same amount of product during these hours as they do in every other hour. If we think of the total amount of output produced during the surplus labor time, it is also free. Marx called this "surplus value," and when the goods or services are sold in the market, this surplus value becomes profits. The source of profits is surplus value, which, in turn, derives from surplus labor time, the root of which is capital's ownership of the non-human means of production and labor's lack of such title. It is the unequal relations of production in capitalism that secure the profits to the owners. Their "skill," "sacrifice," and "entrepreneurship" have nothing to do with it. If Bill Gates were suddenly to go into a permanent coma, his estate would continue to receive Microsoft profits in proportion to his ownership share of the corporation. Profits are unearned.

There are four ways in which profits can be increased. First, as we have seen, they will rise if the working day is lengthened, other things equal. Similar reasoning tells us that profits will fall if the day is shortened. Second, profits will grow if workers labor more intensively during each hour of work, other things being equal (in effect a cut in wages).[6] Third, profits will increase if there is an improvement in technology, such that the amount of labor time needed to produce the subsistence basket of wage goods and services falls. This reduces the necessary (that used up to pay for constant and variable capital) and increases the surplus labor time, thereby increasing profits. Given that there are a fairly large number of products in this basket and that these are produced with the help of a wide range of constant capital, most technological changes will impact the items in the subsistence bundle. Finally, employers will get more profits if they can pay a wage below subsistence. We might call these "super" profits. This has not been an uncommon occurrence in both rich and poor countries, but it has been especially important in the latter. The extraction of such profits will lower the life expectancies of the laborers unless they can find other ways to get food, clothing, and shelter.

Once the C has been converted, in the workplace, into C′, which is final output, and which has a larger value than C (the surplus value), the C′ must be sold. Assuming it is, capital has what it wants, profits. Then the process begins again, driven by relentless competition among capitals. No employer can rest and stop the pursuit of profits; to do so is to eventually perish as a capitalist. Capital must grow, endlessly, or risk death and loss of all the perquisites capital brings with it: political and social power, prestige, abundant consumption, and personal wealth. Accumulation soon outgrows local markets, and the conquest of regional, national, and global markets ensues. Capitalism is, by its nature, an expansionary system, conquering the world and nearly every aspect of our lives.

CLASS STRUGGLE

Before considering the second pillar of capitalism, expropriation, let's look at some implications of capital accumulation. The M–C–C′–M′ model gives us hints about potential clashes between capital and labor. We'll leave aside for now the question of how the working class comes to understand that, despite what appears to be a simple and equal market exchange, they are exploited, in that capital takes their labor time and keeps what they produce without giving them an equivalent in return. Instead, note that there are several possible flash points for labor-capital conflict.

The transformation of money into commodity capital, M to C, always involves the sale of labor power. Disagreements can arise around this sale over wage rates, hours, benefits, and working conditions. Unless the labor-power sellers are collectively organized, rarely will they have much leverage in negotiating a better deal than the employer offers. Only those with unique skills in high demand, such as professional athletes, musicians, actors, scientists, and the like, will be able to command what they want in the labor market. But if workers have formed a labor union, then their union can negotiate more advantageous outcomes. If they are organized politically, they might win legislation mandating minimum wages, maximum hours, safe working conditions, national health insurance, retirement pensions, decent labor laws, disability insurance, unemployment compensation, as well as a commitment to full employment.

The production of output, the combining of K and V (the C in our formula) to create C′, brings labor and capital into more direct potential conflicts. Here, what is good for labor is inimical to capital. And it is here that workers directly encounter one another and can begin to see their potential power. This is where the impetus for collective struggle takes hold and solidarity is realized. Union organizing campaigns, slowdowns, strikes of all kinds, factory occupations, picketing, sabotage of equipment, and a host of other actions originate in the labor process. Not only wages and hours, but the speed of assembly lines, the pace of office work, the attempts by management to minimize the time and motions needed to complete a task, the introduction of new technology, the employer's financial data, the decision to close or move a plant, the speech rights of employees—all might be bones of contention. Time is money for the workers, too, and much more than that, as demonstrated in the 1880s during mass agitations in the United

States for the eight-hour day, when marching throngs shouted, "8 hours for work, 8 hours for sleep, 8 hours for what we will!"

While the C' embodies surplus value, profits cannot be made until the C' is sold in the marketplace. Profits must be realized. Workers intent on winning concessions from their employers might try to prevent the sale of the output. They could do this by blocking trucks, trains, planes, or ships, disrupting electronic networks, picketing businesses (for example, wholesalers) that purchase or sell the company's goods or services. They can ask the public to show solidarity by boycotting their employer's product. And they can elicit support from other unions to honor their picket lines or have their own members refuse to make deliveries or load transport vehicles. They could even try to generate a general strike, like the one the International Longshore Workers Union (ILWU) brought about in San Francisco in 1934.[7]

Finally, as capitalism bursts national boundaries, global working-class organizations might form, or union and other labor groups in one country might act in support of those in another part of the world. History is replete with examples. The Communication Workers of America (CWA) has a longstanding tradition of global solidarity, as do unions in many nations.[8] The more worldwide capital becomes, with increasingly complex supply chains and financing, the more laborers in any country can disrupt the accumulation of capital in one or many other places.

THE RESERVE ARMY OF LABOR

Conflicts over exploitation are constrained by an important element in endless capital accumulation, what Marx termed a "reserve army of labor," a pool of people not working for wages that can be drawn into paid labor when needed. Several elements intrinsic to capital accumulation create this army. To produce products cheaper and to enhance managerial control, employers divide work into simple component parts. By doing so, they de-skill the work once done by craft workers. This automatically increases the number of hands who can perform the labor, since what needs to be done now are subtasks. Early factories were thus able to employ children and women. The latter were capable of doing skilled tasks, but they had been denied this because of their gender. The augmented pool of available workers formed a reserve army of labor that could undermine the wages and conditions of the employed. Desperation could make those needing employment undercut the position of those with work.

To reinforce the de-skilling begun by the division of jobs and to replace workers, capital began to introduce machinery, which not only augmented the reserve army of labor, but also spawned perpetual churning of it. This made the employed insecure, because machinery stood ready to replace them, especially if they had won higher wages, shorter hours, and better working conditions.[9] In the United States today, the wages of some farm laborers have been rising considerably due to the government's draconian harassment of immigrants, which has reduced the supply of workers. In response, grape growers are now beginning to introduce advanced mechanization to prune and harvest their vines.[10]

As capital moves beyond national boundaries, workers in the home country can be replaced by less expensive labor abroad. After the North American Free Trade Agreement (NAFTA) was implemented in 1994, U.S. businesses flocked to Mexico, closing factories in the United States, increasing the reserve army here. At the same time, the agreement allowed the tax-free export of cheap U.S. corn to Mexico. This drove Mexican corn farmers out of business—a form of expropriation—forcing them to leave the land and migrate to cities in Mexico and the United States, making the surplus workforce larger in both countries.[11] Globally, there are 244 million migrants; some remain in their home nations, while others travel from one part of the Global South to another, with the rest traveling to the Global North.

What the reserve army does is place limits on the victories workers can win within the confines of capitalism. We will trace out the implications of this when we try to answer the question: Can the working class change the world?

EXPROPRIATION

Primitive Accumulation. Although both markets and workplaces are central to the functioning of capitalism, it is important to understand that these are embedded in a larger society. Our focus is limited if we ignore this and concentrate only on what is normally considered the economic dimension of the system. Expropriation is another word for theft, for the taking of something that is not your right to take. It is distinguished from appropriation, which, in our context, simply means using something. All human societies must appropriate land to live. We can call this property, but it is not private property until it is expropriated. With capitalism, land was routinely stolen. In feudal Europe, serfs had the right to use common lands, those that were neither the fields of the lord nor the plots of the serfs. These lands were used for grazing animals, gathering firewood and plant food, hunting, and fishing. Lords, often in league with merchants and always supported by governments, began to deny peasants their customary appropriation of the commons. In England, the Black Act of 1723 made many formerly legal actions, such as cutting down a tree for firewood on common land, capital crimes.[12]

Expropriation has been critical to capital's development, and it interacts with and usually reinforces accumulation, although it can at times be a substitute for accumulation. As shown by many scholars, Marx foremost among them, the origin of capitalism was riddled with expropriation. As Marx put it, in contesting the notion that the intelligence, diligence, and frugality of a select few gave rise to the new mode of production: "In actual history, it is a notorious fact that conquest, enslavement, robbery, murder, in short, force, play the greatest part."[13] The land was forcibly converted into private property, the serfs evicted either directly or through the raising of rents, far above their traditional level and payable not in kind but in money. This had the fortunate effect, from capital's perspective, of creating a class of persons "free" of any means of production and therefore compelled to sell their labor power to someone who owned such means. Here we see how expropriation and exploitation are intertwined. Merchants and lords expropriated the land from the serfs, who then were driven into wage labor, to be exploited by capitalists.

Similarly, indigenous people fell victim to land theft as the great powers of Europe began their conquest and colonization of the Americas, Africa, the rest of Europe, and Asia. In what is now Mexico and South America, Indians were dragooned to work in mines, the wealth of which was then shipped to Europe, mainly England, fueling the accumulation of capital. Where the indigenous populations were exterminated or ravaged by diseases brought by the foreigners, slaves, dark-skinned and largely from Africa, were kidnapped and shipped under deplorable conditions across the Atlantic Ocean to spend their lives tormented and tortured on plantations growing tobacco, sugar, and cotton. This was an expropriation of the human body itself, with the labor power of the slaves paid nothing but exploited nonetheless, generating enormous profits for their masters. Slave labor producing cotton made possible the burgeoning growth of capitalism's quintessential infant industry, textiles, the development of which solidified the preeminence of the new mode of production, not only in England and the United States but in the world. The wombs of women slaves were likewise expropriated to satisfy the lusts of slaveowners and to help maintain, through giving birth, a further supply of slaves. There were slaves who were not black, but skin color was an obvious physical marker, and the slave trade brought some eight million black slaves to the "New World." Given that the slave owners and colonizers were overwhelmingly white, and given that they had already expropriated and partially exterminated indigenous peoples, an ideology of the superiority of whites and the inferiority of blacks, as well as Indians and later Chinese, was inevitable.

Slavery and Racism. Capitalism from its beginning was racialized, with profound consequences for the development of the world's working classes. First, a racial capitalism gave employers a critical wedge against interracial solidarity. In the southern United States, for example, whites were chosen as overseers and for slave patrols that chased after those who had escaped from bondage. After the Civil War, whites became law enforcement officers, chain gang overseers, and prison guards in the Jim Crow system that reversed the gains of Reconstruction and reinstated a slave-like terrorism and peonage on the black population. Former slaves were arrested on trumped-up charges and then leased to employers as convict labor. Throughout the country, the long period of demonization and denigration of slaves as ignorant, childlike, and in need of white supervision and guidance helped to create a white working class that was racist and unwilling to join with black workers in confrontations with employers.[14] Remarkably, historian Robin D. G. Kelley has shown that in Alabama during the Great Depression of the 1930s, there was considerable race prejudice among white members of the Communist Party, which was emphatic about the establishment of a black nation in the southern Black Belt:

A former member of the Socialist Party who joined the Communists in 1930 argued that if the Party concentrated exclusively on whites, "they would carry the whole South" in the elections. This was not just a tactical suggestion, however. After the proletarian revolution, he explained, black people "would have to be disciplined for 50 years, since the Negro has just emerged from serfdom." Needless to say, the author of this letter was summarily expelled.[15]

There are many examples of white workers making common cause with black and other racial and ethnic groups, but serious examination of the history of the rich capitalist nations shows that racial conflict has always been a daunting impediment to working-class unity. In the United States and elsewhere, slaves revolted. Black workers protested, struck, marched, boycotted, and demanded full political rights. Had whites fully and aggressively supported these efforts, employers and the capitalist system would have faced a formidable enemy.

Second, the expropriation of black bodies, and those of all who have been enslaved, along with the racist attitudes and structures that ensued, made it possible, when slavery was abolished, to pay wage laborers from these groups below-subsistence wages. This increased surplus value and generated extra profits, some of which could be shared with white workers, giving them a stake in the continuation of racism. We can call this "super exploitation" or another form of expropriation, the latter because black workers are not paid the value of their labor power.

Invariably, racial minorities—or sometimes majorities as in the case of South Africa during apartheid—were assigned the worst jobs, with the lowest wages. To the extent that whites bought the idea that low wages were a sign of low productivity or defective intelligence, once again racism was reinforced.

Third, the divide-and-rule strategy allows capitalists to pay lower wages than they might otherwise have to provide for white employees. Had all workers joined in opposition to their bosses, they might have forced capital to pay them higher wages, reduce hours, provide better benefits, and supply improved working conditions. Once more, the expropriation of black bodies leads to greater exploitation, this time of white workers. too.

Fourth, the expropriation of black bodies continued after slavery ended. What else was contract labor except the theft of black labor? The Jim Crow period in the United States saw the robbery of agricultural property that some former slaves had gained during Reconstruction. Much later, after the early success of the civil rights movement, black workers managed to gain a foothold in northern unionized manufacturing plants. When economic stagnation took hold in the early 1970s, the industrial heartland turned into the Rust Belt, and those hardest hit were the black workers last hired or promoted.

As governments at all levels implemented austerity policies, beginning in the 1970s, unemployment and poverty rose most in black communities. Segregated housing made it difficult for people to move, and there was little public help in terms of housing, job training, better schools, and health care. A war on drugs was declared, aimed at black (and Native American and Hispanic) America. The results were ugly, especially in the startling rise in African American imprisonment. Black bodies were now entombed in prison cells, subject to repeated physical and mental torture. However, capital has profited handsomely from this burgeoning prison-industrial complex, making profits on everything from extortionist phone charges to private prisons, food services, uniforms, prison construction, and prison labor. A massive network of lawyers, prosecutors, judges, parole officers, and counselors have also benefited, along with white workers servicing the system, especially the heavily unionized prison guards. Unscrupulous, ambitious politicians have also preyed upon black minds and bodies, accusing those imprisoned of being evil predators and their families as enablers.

The enslavement of Africans in the seventeenth and eighteenth centuries took place as England, Holland, Spain, and Portugal invaded, colonized, and began production in the rest of the world. This brutal process meant the expropriation of enormous areas of land and the mineral resources under them, not to mention expropriating the bodies of the indigenous people enslaved. Parts of the European populations that could not be absorbed in the original merchant-capitalist enterprises, largely in the textile industry, were encouraged or impressed into military service to help in the conquests. They were also persuaded to emigrate to the colonies, and money was made even on this as travel funds were borrowed against an obligation to labor for capital in the new foreign outposts. These primarily white settlers could be used as servants, but also as overseers for slaves, making the racialization of capitalism that much easier. All this expropriation swelled the wealth of capital, giving its owners the means to industrialize and exploit workers on a new, higher level.

Colonialism and Imperialism. Although there were rebellions in the colonies of England, Spain, Portugal, France, and Holland, except in Haiti, independence was not achieved in the colonies until the twentieth century. However, the infiltration of capital had so deformed the economies and people in the colonies, and so powerful were the militaries of the rich countries, that political independence did not mean economic independence. What the late *Monthly Review* editor Harry Magdoff called "imperialism without colonies" kept the newly independent nations tethered to their former overlords and to the new hegemonic global power, the United States. Instead of direct military control, now the global market, always rewarding those with the most economic power, kept profits flowing from what we now call the Global South to the Global North.[16] Aiding and abetting global capital are a subordinate class of capitalists in the Global South, people and businesses that oversee the exploitation and expropriation of peasants and workers. This local capital is permitted to keep some of the spoils, just as white workers have been allowed to share in some of the profits generated by the super-exploitation of black and other nonwhite workers. In modern-day imperialism, military power is held in reserve, used whenever a country tries to assert real independence. In fact, the new imperialism has seen an unprecedented explosion of military spending and an insane buildup of nuclear weapons.

The split between rich and poor countries, between Global North and South, once again shows the importance of both expropriation and exploitation and how they are connected. Not only have the expropriations, especially of peasant land, augmented wealth, they have provided a basis for future exploitation, for example in industrial agriculture and mining. The potential number of people involved is in the billions, creating a landless class that will have to make a living somehow. Such a large pool of prospective laborers puts considerable downward pressure on wages, meaning that capital can pay below subsistence wages, generating above-average profits. States in nations rich and poor have shown an increasing willingness to sell public property to private businesses, another form of expropriation and yet another opportunity for future exploitation. It should be noted as well that the property taken can be used as collateral for bank loans, which can serve as money capital.

Governments have actively participated in modern-day theft of peasant land, almost always in the service of private capital. India may be the poster child for state-sanctioned land seizures. As Indian journalist Bernard D'Mello writes:

> The LAA [Land Acquisition Act] of 1894 and the Forest Act of 1927 remained in independent India under Article 372 of the Constitution, which smoothed the incorporation of colonial era laws. Indeed, the LAA of 1894 was amended in 1962 to give greater powers to the state to characterize a whole range of infrastructural and industrial projects as serving the "public purpose," and in 1984 to make it even easier to acquire land for private companies. Any activity of the state was now deemed to serve the "public purpose," as also almost any activity of private companies.[17]

Capital's lust for export-crop lands and mineral wealth in India is so great and the remarkable unity of interests between business and the state so tight, with startling instances of corruption and police and paramilitary violence, that large swathes of land have been confiscated and tens of millions of peasants displaced just in the past thirty years.

Just as slavery divided workers within a country, colonial conquest and imperialism split working classes between those in oppressed and oppressor countries. The same rationalizations were made for the expropriation of land and labor, just as the super-exploitation of workers in the Global South was used to justify the oppression of slaves and emancipated black workers. The Global South comprises billions of nonwhite people, so little wonder that immigrants from these regions are treated so poorly in the wealthy, and white, powers of the Global North. No wonder that U.S. president Donald Trump has dismissed these human beings as criminals, rapists, and inhabitants of "shithole countries." The plunder of wealth and the repugnant treatment of workers in the poor countries by the rich nations—and not so poor in the case of China, at least in terms of per capita production—is continual as their corporations work together to solidify the worldwide power of capital.

Patriarchy. For a social system to survive, women must give birth to children and nurture them. For children to become adults, they must be cared for by their parents, other adults, and the larger society. One way that societies can be described is by the degree of patriarchy. For most of our time on earth, we produced and distributed life's necessities without a rigid hierarchy, in gathering and hunting bands. Classes did not exist, and egalitarian relations of production prevailed. Patriarchy, though not nonexistent, was mild by comparison with what followed. In pre-capitalist class societies, patriarchy was more pronounced. However, women were an integral part of production. We have seen that the bodies of women who were slaves in colonial societies were expropriated by white, male slaveowners, raped and used for breeding an increasing supply of their human chattel. Yet women were at the center of slave families and worked side-by-side with men in the fields. In feudal society, as in all peasant communities, women and men jointly produced the household needs and the goods that had to be transferred as rent to their lords. To an outside observer, these arrangements would be transparent.

Matters changed dramatically with capitalism. Before the advent of factories, production was still a family enterprise, carried on in the home of the artisan. Once factory production began, employers hired women and children, which not only wore down the bodies of the new factory hands, but also disrupted families, making it nearly impossible to maintain social life. As Nancy Fraser tells us, in analyzing the changes wrought by capitalism:

One is the epistemic shift from production to social reproduction—the forms of provisioning, caregiving and interaction that produce and maintain social bonds. Variously called "care," "affective labour," or "subjectivation," this activity forms capitalism's human subjects, sustaining them as embodied natural beings, while also constituting them as social beings, forming their habitus and the socio-ethical substance, or *Sittlichkeit*, in which they move. Central here is the work of socializing the young, building communities, producing and reproducing the shared meanings, affective dispositions and horizons of value that underpin social cooperation. In capitalist societies much, though not all, of this activity goes on outside the market, in households, neighbourhoods and a host of public institutions, including schools and childcare centres; and much of it, though not all, does not take the form of wage labour. Yet social-reproductive activity is absolutely necessary to the existence of waged work, the accumulation of surplus value and the functioning of capitalism as such. Wage labour could not exist in the absence of housework, child-raising, schooling, affective care and a host of other activities which help to produce new generations of workers and replenish existing ones, as well as to maintain social bonds and shared understandings. Much like "original accumulation," therefore, social reproduction is an indispensable background condition for the possibility of capitalist production.[18]

In the early factory system, women and children were so severely exploited that the labor supply itself faced diminution. This, along with social protest, eventually led to laws limiting child labor and the kinds of work women could do. A sharp separation took shape between production and social reproduction, with men the family's main breadwinners and women relegated to overseers of the household. What the women did was essential to the production of wage laborers; without it, capital accumulation was impossible. Yet they became increasingly invisible. In effect, capital had expropriated their labor, obtaining it free of charge, lowering costs of production. Along with this split came an ethos that professed the naturalness of women's subordination to men. Religious ideologues pronounced this the will of God, and laws sanctioned it. Women typically could not own property or vote.

Women, especially those who were poor, never stopped working for wages. However, they faced considerable labor market discrimination and hostility from male co-workers. They were subject to sexual abuse as well. Men too often believed that women's place was in the home, bearing and raising children. The critical social reproduction labor women performed, whether they worked for wages or not, was debased and degraded, even as it was expropriated by capital. Women not in the labor force also became members of the reserve army of labor, drawn into the labor force when needed and expelled when not. It is interesting to read propaganda glorifying the role of women during the Second World War. The heroic image of Rosie the Riveter portrayed women as strong and capable of doing work that had previously been the province for men.[19] But when the war ended, they were expelled from the workforce and expected to resume their role as homemakers.

The Environment. Humans must appropriate nature to survive. Gatherers and hunters did this in such a way that nature was almost always constantly restored, kept healthy so that its productiveness could be maintained. With class societies, disharmonies between us and the natural world developed. In ancient Greece's slave-based production, there was considerable deforestation and desalination.[20] However, capital's incessant drive to accumulate capital has brought with it a destruction of nature unknown in earlier modes of production. First, it has taken the air, soil, and water as "free" resources, to use as it pleases. We have seen how land was expropriated and then used with wage labor to produce food. Little concern was evinced for the health of the soil, which, as greater output from it was demanded, began to lose its nutrients. In rural societies what was consumed was done so locally, and human waste was returned to the soil. Capitalism drove people out of rural areas when it expropriated their land. Large agglomerations of human beings came to live in cities, where human and animal wastes were dumped in rivers and streams, not only generating epidemics and polluting the water but denying the soil its natural nutrients.[21] Capital sought technological and imperial solutions, developing chemical fertilizers and scouring the world for fertilizers such as guano from the islands off the coast of Peru and bones from catacombs and battlefields. But though these fertilizers increased production, they ran up against limits to the elasticity of soil and its capacity to yield more output even as its constituent elements were depleted. Eventually, more and more fertilizer had to be added to a given amount of land. The chemicals in the fertilizers leached into the water, killing fish and creating dead zones in our oceans.

We have, then, a final example of the interplay between expropriation and exploitation. Nature is stolen by capital, so that labor can be further exploited. In addition, land, water, even air, are made into commodities that can be bought and sold, again creating new arenas for accumulation. The social costs of capital's abuse of nature is typically borne by workers and peasants. They live where air pollution is worst, where the soil has been most degraded. They drink contaminated water.[22] Their workplaces and their hunting and fishing grounds are fouled in multiple ways. When floods, hurricanes, and droughts, caused and exacerbated by capitalist-induced global warming, descend upon humanity, the least of us suffer most.

Expropriation Struggles. Just as exploitation brings forth possibilities for conflict between labor and capital, so too does expropriation spawn the potential for class struggles. These have often been neglected by those whose focus has been on exploitation in the workplace. This viewpoint can be characterized as a class-first approach. That is, it is presumed that there is a working class with universal needs and meeting them must be privileged if we are to empower the class. An emphasis on race, gender, nature, and imperialism distracts from the class struggle. We saw this in the United States from many of the left-wing supporters of Bernie Sanders for U.S. president. They said that the key to the campaign should be universal programs like full employment and national healthcare. They argued that these would benefit black and other minority groups the most because they were the poorest. What this missed is that capitalism has been racialized, gendered, and wasteful of nature from its inception. Racism, patriarchy, and environmental catastrophe must be addressed directly. In other words, there can be no separation between exploitation and expropriation.[23]

If we embrace this perspective, many struggles take on a new light. If every effort to end exploitation is either implicitly or explicitly anti-capitalist, then so is every movement to end patriarchy, racism, and the rift between humans and nature. These are not just peripheral to capitalism; they are intrinsic to it. They cannot be eliminated within capitalism but only in a new, radically different society.

Capital will always try to co-opt attempts to limit, much less end, exploitation and expropriation. There are countless examples of this, from corrupt and employer-friendly labor unions to the subservient embrace of white rule in the United States by Booker T. Washington. Some feminists simply want more women CEOs and members of Congress. And some environmentalists have been willing to make compromises with business that end up doing nothing to end environmental destruction. But these do not constrain the accumulation of capital or liberate all black people, all women, and all of nature from capital's rule. However, all crusades to make freedom, substantive equality, and real democracy reality are, by definition, radically anti-capitalist. This will be further discussed in the final chapter.

CRITICAL INSTITUTIONS

All economic systems need structures that allow them to continue to exist. In feudalism, the Catholic religion played a critical role, with its instruction that the serf owed obedience to the feudal lord, on pain of eternal hellfire. In both feudalism and slavery, the force of the lord and the slaveowner, their ability to torture and kill the serf or the slave without consequence, served as a powerful mechanism for the reproduction of class inequality and exploitation.

The State. Capitalism is a complex and opaque system, so, as is the case with the unpaid time of wage laborers and the many types of expropriation, the institutions that underpin and rationalize this mode of production require some effort to penetrate. The most important is the state. Capitalism was born inside state structures. One of the first things King Henry VIII of England did after breaking with the Catholic Church was to confiscate the Church's properties, which included many monasteries and other properties with arable land. Henry then sold land to rich merchants, who began a process of enclosure, evicting serfs and converting farms to the production of wool for sale in the growing textile market. Governments from the beginning used their police power to protect private property and combat rebellions by peasants and workers. They enacted laws guaranteeing ownership of property, enforcing contracts, and many other matters important to capital. They have sanctioned slavery and the rankest kinds of discrimination against minority groups. They have denied women the right to vote.[24]

States have also developed means to steady markets in times of crisis, and they have enacted legislation that grants working people some concessions while strictly limiting or forbidding actions that could threaten the existence of capital. The first evolved from the ideas of the British economist John Maynard Keynes. Since the end of the Second World War, and in some countries like Sweden, before the war, capitalist governments have maintained high and generally growing levels of spending, providing a crucial prop to overall consumption and investment. This helps maintain the demand for goods and services, stabilizing the economy.[25] The second arose in the face of political agitation emanating from the working class, forcing states to make concessions that placed some limits on the actions of capital, but not enough to threaten its power. In the United States, the National Labor Relations Act of 1935 is a case in point. This statute gave unprecedented rights to organize unions and bargain collectively with employers. It was bitterly opposed by employers, and over time the courts and amendments watered it down severely. But even the original act excluded the largely black agriculture and domestic labor sectors of the workforce.[26]

One of the characteristics of capitalism is the separation of the political and economic spheres. In the feudal mode of production, state and economy were controlled directly by the nobility. They sat atop the manors, where food, cloth, and artisanal goods were produced; and they controlled politics as well. With capitalism, however, at least in those organized as liberal democracies, political leaders are elected by those eligible to vote. For capital's ideologues, this is the definition of democracy and the reason why they claim that capitalism and democracy are congruent. The notion has been spread far and wide, and, to the extent that most people believe it, obscures the autocracy that reigns supreme in the workplace.

Marx and Engels wrote in the *Communist Manifesto*: "The executive of the modern state is but a committee for managing the common affairs of the whole bourgeoisie."[27] That is, capitalists are always in competition with one another, and on their own they could not forge a common strategy with respect to matters from economic relations with the rest of the world to an organized working class. Therefore, the state takes this responsibility. Given the complexity and extent of this, modern states encompass a panoply of departments, regulatory agencies, courts, military, intelligence organs, diplomats, and an army of employees. Part of the state apparatus has responsibility for doing things that protect employees, the environment, health, and the like. This means that there are spaces in the state machinery for mass actions to pressure governments to enact measures that improve the lives of working-class people.

History, however, has shown the truth of the definition of Marx and Engels. The default position of governments in capitalist societies is to serve the interests of capital. It does this as a matter of course most of the time, through legislatures, laws, and its budget (taxes and spending). But when required, its instinct is for repression, violence, war when necessary. These days, the weak democracy through which capital rules is fraying around the world.[28] One sign of this is the weakening of the separation between polity and economy, replaced by the direct rule of capital. Business still has enormous leverage over the state through its financing and purchasing of government bonds and its campaign contributions. But now capitalists often rule more openly, as elected and appointed state officers and as financiers of what had formerly been public programs, both national and global. Another word for the direct political rule of capital is fascism, whose ugly head has been raised in many countries, including Austria, Hungary, Poland, India, and the United States.[29]

Schooling and Media. Two other critical institutions are schooling and media. As modern nation-states were formed, the elites who wielded power saw the need to forge national identities. Disparate ethnic and regional groups did not think of themselves as French or Italian or German, so one solution to the problem this created—for example, the need to make people more loyal to the nation than to their social class—was mandatory education, provided in both public and private schools. In nearly every nation, young people were legally mandated to attend school for a minimum number of years. This made children forced consumers of whatever their instructors told them. Schools, although they did teach literacy and basic mathematical skills, spent much effort instilling both patriotism and a positive view of capitalism. In addition, a hierarchy of schools was constructed, with the best schools, those that offered some critical education, reserved for those families with money. Colleges and universities, which predated capitalism, were greatly expanded, again with a wealth-based hierarchy, and, until the post–Second World War period, student bodies that excluded the poor and most ethnic and racial minorities.

Given that working men and women, including former slaves, wanted their children to have access to education, struggles over schools, how they were controlled and what they taught, have been common. Victories have been achieved, at all levels of schooling, including higher education. But overall, success in school tracks closely with success at work. That is, the criteria for good grades in school are much the same as those that win workers high evaluations from their supervisors. Teachers who step outside of education's propaganda mission soon find themselves unemployed or marginalized. Nonetheless, it is not impossible to get a first-class education in capitalist countries, although it is no mean feat to do so.[30]

A major claim for education is that it is the key to solving myriad social problems, from low wages and poverty to inequality. This helps deflect attention from the economic inequity inherent in capitalism. Interestingly, despite ample evidence that education has little effect on the many injustices the system causes, the claim for the efficacy of schooling lives on, which is proof that education serves to reinforce capital's power.[31]

While education, in addition to its socializing function, is itself a site for considerable capital accumulation (textbooks, standardized tests, the selling of research patents by universities, for-profit colleges), mainstream media are capital-accumulating enterprises as well. As such, they depend on corporate advertising, and their goal is to turn a profit. They have a cozy relationship with the state, and the government is one of their primary sources of information. Seldom do the media either name or analyze critically the mode of production in which they operate. This is not to say that what they publish, or broadcast, never provides useful information. But if we look at television news, for example, endless commentary assaults viewers with the trivia of politics and celebrity culture. "Experts" are typically political hacks or former military personnel. In some cases, like Fox News in the United States, right-wing, neo-fascist propaganda is the order of the day. With print media, even the best newspapers, such as the *New York Times*, seldom stray from a narrow discourse, a generally centrist politics that excludes radical analyses of capitalism. Journalists engage in self-censorship, knowing in advance what is acceptable and what is not.[32]

The pro-capitalist bias of the media is exceptionally clear when we scrutinize coverage of state enemies. Even a cursory look at U.S. media reporting on the affairs of countries such as Cuba, Russia (and especially the Soviet Union), China under Mao, North Korea, and Venezuela shows the most astonishing prejudices. The United States tried repeatedly to assassinate Fidel Castro, imposed internationally illegal economic embargoes, poisoned crops, and engaged in massive psychological warfare and misinformation campaigns against Cuba. These facts are ignored by media, but no chance is missed to declare the island a police state. Much the same can be said about coverage of Venezuela and many other nations.[33]

As media have migrated to the internet, critics of mainstream outlets have claimed that it has become possible for those with limited resources to provide a wider range of views, including deeper analyses of capitalism. There is truth in this, and there are many possibilities that weren't available before. However, those with the most wealth have had the greatest influence on what we get electronically. And talented journalists have had a difficult time earning a living on the World Wide Web.[34]

Capitalism's supporting institutions combine to make it appear that capitalism is what it is not. It is the realm of freedom, democracy, the best we can hope for. As former British prime minister Margaret Thatcher was fond of saying, "There is no alternative." If in our schools, from our media, from our governments, even from the pulpits of our churches, we hear repeatedly that we live in the best of all possible worlds, our minds are conditioned to believe this. An ideology predisposed to take the system as given and unchangeable creates a powerful barrier to radical change.

CAPITALISM IS A HEGEMONIC social order. Capital seeks to dominate as many aspects of our lives as possible and to control every institution, from state to schools. Very little escapes its domination, including our thoughts. Its two essential underpinnings are exploitation of wage labor and the expropriation of nature, the non-market labor of women, and the bodies of black and other minority people. A complex set of structures supports these. Is it possible for capital's chief antagonist, the working class, to combat and defeat it? We shall see.

3—Nothing to Lose but Their Chains

"The proletarians have nothing to lose but their chains. They have a world to win. Proletarians of All Countries, Unite!" These are the final three sentences of *The Manifesto of the Communist Party*, better known simply as the *Communist Manifesto*, published in 1848, and written the year before by Karl Marx and Frederick Engels.[1] The words are a stirring rallying cry for working men and women to join in revolt against a social order that keeps them in chains, and then collectively build a better, freer world. The year 1848 was one of radical revolt throughout Europe, and the two revolutionaries were hopeful that capitalism would soon end and that upon its ashes a new society could be constructed. In chapter 2, we looked at the points of possible contention between labor and capital as well as some of the impediments to working-class unity and revolt. We will do some of this again here, but we will first see why Marx and Engels saw workers as the agents of radical change.

THE RISE OF THE WORKING CLASS

Let's examine the famous exhortation penned by Marx and Engels. First, proletarians are wage laborers, members of one of the two great social classes in the capitalist mode of production, the other being the capitalists who employ them. We learned in chapter 2 that because workers own no or not enough means of production, they cannot survive unless they sell their labor power to employers. Marx believed, correctly, that as capitalism developed, wage labor would become the overwhelmingly dominant form of work. When capitalism was in its infancy in the sixteenth and seventeenth centuries, there were many other types of work arrangements because several modes of production coexisted: gathering and hunting, slavery, and various tributary systems such as feudalism. All but gatherers and hunters labored under coercive conditions, ruled by slave owners or feudal lords. Capitalism gradually undermined its feudal predecessor, breaking the direct, personal, and highly unequal relationship that existed between the lords who controlled the rural estates and the serfs who did the work. Land became private property, and again as we saw in chapter 2, serfs were forced from the land and into the wage labor force, either in the towns and cities or on sheep farms in the countryside. In both town and country, many former serfs were unemployed.

Although feudalism declined as capitalism grew, the same cannot be said for slavery.[2] As historian Gerald Horne has shown, there was a vibrant market for slaves throughout the Middle Ages in Europe, Eurasia, and the Arab world. And as Horne and others have shown, slavery and capitalism were intimately connected. From the beginning, the brutal treatment of slaves by profit-seeking slave owners was racialized, to distinguish those who were slaves and typically of darker skin color from those who were "white." Capitalism, then, and especially in the Americas and Europe, was a racialized capitalism.

Second, Marx and Engels say that "proletarians have nothing to lose but their chains. They have a world to win." Here, they imply by their words that they believe there is something special about these proletarians. Human beings have existed for at least 100,000 years, and perhaps, as some archaeologists now believe, much longer. This means that for probably 90 to 95 percent of our time on earth, humans lived in relatively small bands, living by gathering nuts, berries, and plants, supplemented whenever possible by meat from hunted animals. The production of life's necessities, as well as their distribution, was carried out in a remarkably egalitarian way, without permanent leaders and without the division of skilled tasks, like making tools or clothing, into unskilled details or subtasks. Gatherers and hunters eventually populated most of the earth, an astonishing achievement for those that modernists call "primitive."

Sharp changes in social organization arose once humans learned to cultivate plants. Over a long period of time, sedentary agriculture began to replace gathering and hunting, and along with it came the division of society into classes. Farming allowed the production of a surplus above basic needs, and this in turn made possible the existence of people who performed a social role but did no work. Feudal lords, emperors, priests, slave owners, and the like marked pre-capitalist class society, and these men (and some women) were able to use their positions of relative leisure and access to the surplus of production to exert power over the peasants, serfs, and slaves who performed the necessary tasks of producing output. Though there was great variability in class structures, the most basic commonality was the direct and personal relationship between exploiters and exploited.

Capitalism radically transformed class society. In place of personal, direct relationships between those who controlled production and those who did not, the new system's relations of production were mediated by an impersonal market. Today, it is uncommon for workers to know the owners of the enterprises that employ them, not just personally but even to recognize their names, and it is rare for consumers to know who made the things they purchase. What is more, the extraction of the surplus value from the efforts of those who toil in factories, mines, mills, offices, and the multitude of other capitalist businesses is hidden by the market. It appears that we workers are paid a wage determined by the impersonal forces of supply and demand. It isn't obvious that we are being exploited, that a surplus created by us has somehow become the property of the owner. We don't appear to be in the same position as a serf who could have been seen delivering part of the family's crop to the lord. Much less are we similar to slaves, whose very bodies are owned by the masters. We are not tied by the threat of violence or even death to a lord or master but are free to work for anyone who will hire us. How is it, then, that we have nothing to lose but our chains?

To grasp Marx and Engels's meaning, it is necessary to understand just how radical capitalism is. Of great significance is the fact that it is the first economic system in which there is an inherent growth imperative. We know that the goal of every capitalist is to accumulate capital. What compels this and makes growth necessary is competition among capitals. A business either succeeds in growing or it dies. The search for profitable markets drives employers to discover new products, new markets, everywhere and anywhere. From local to national to global, that is capital's trajectory. Today, there is barely a part of our lives, from birth to death, or any part of the world where capital has failed to penetrate. As this has happened, global business gets divided into a relatively small number of great capitals, owned in large part by a tiny fraction of the world's people. The enterprises employ an enormous class of persons who must sell their ability to work to them. Businesses, aided and abetted by governments, force small farmers, peasants, and local businesses out of the marketplace and into wage labor. The development of capitalism creates an ever-larger group of wage workers and makes alternatives to this mode of being either less appealing or unlikely to bear fruit.

Inside workplaces, equally dramatic changes occur. As all successful employers know, the key to generating profits is to control, as absolutely as possible, every aspect of their business. And nothing is more critical than the command of the workers, because they are the main active agents in production. By control, we mean the ways in which workers interact with one another and with the tools and machines they utilize. These interactions comprise the *labor process*, and it is this that must be ruled. Historically, many and varied methods of controlling the labor process have been implemented. Let us look at some of the most important techniques, each of which reduced the influence over production that workers could exert.

First came centralization. In England, for example, the production of woven wool cloth initially took place in the weavers' homes, with raw wool and sometimes looms supplied by wool merchants. The wool would be worked up into cloth and the finished product returned to the merchant for a price per unit. The merchant would then endeavor to sell the woven cloth. While this way of making cloth (and many other products), known as the outworking or putting-out system, was profitable and allowed merchants to pit one group of weavers against others in bidding wars, it didn't allow sufficient control by the owners of the wool. It was difficult for them to prevent theft through the making of inferior cloth, and it thwarted the use of machinery. To get around these problems, employers began to recruit workers into factories, usually one-story buildings in which labor was carried on as usual but now came under the direct supervision of the owners or their hired managers. A whistle could sound the call to work, and punishments could be meted out to latecomers. Theft would be discouraged by the watchful eyes of foremen. The larger scale of production implicit in factories also made machinery economically viable.

Centralization made it possible for supervisors to observe how skilled weavers and other artisans performed their labor. They began to see that these craftsmen divided their task into subtasks or details. Harry Braverman described such labor division in the making of a metal funnel:

> For example, a tinsmith makes a funnel: he draws the elevation view on sheetmetal, and from this develops the outline of an unrolled funnel and its bottom spout. He then cuts out each piece with snips and shears, rolls it to its proper shape, and crimps or rivets the seams. He then rolls the top edge, solders

the seams, solders on a hanging ring, washes away the acid used in soldering, and rounds the funnel to its final shape.

But when he applies the same process to a quantity of identical funnels, his mode of operation changes. Instead of laying out the work directly on the material, he makes a pattern and uses it to mark off the total quantity of funnels needed; then he cuts them all out, one after the other, rolls them, etc. In this case, instead of making a single funnel in the course of an hour or two, he spends hours or even days on each step of the process, creating in each case fixtures, clamps, devices, etc., which would not be worth making for a single funnel but which, where a sufficiently large quantity of funnels is to be made, speed each step sufficiently so that the saving justifies the extra outlay of time. Quantities, he has discovered, will be produced with less trouble and greater economy of time in this way than by finishing each funnel individually before starting the next.[3]

It was but a short step from managerial observation of what the craftsman did to deducing that it would be much cheaper to assign unskilled laborers to perform the separate details repetitively over the course of the workday. The key was to economize on the use of skilled, more expensive labor. Inventor and engineer Charles Babbage systematically explained this in his book *On the Economy of Machinery and Manufactures,*[4] so Braverman coined this as the Babbage Principle.[5] Not only did it greatly cheapen production; it also enhanced the employer's control over the labor process by making workers relatively interchangeable and easily replaced. It was even possible for factory owners to employ children to do repetitive tasks.

Both centralization and the detailed division of labor gave a sharp impetus to mechanization, which in turn further enhanced capital's control, both by making the pace of production determined by machines and by further de-skilling work.[6] Frederick Taylor, the celebrated guru of management control, was able, as a consequence of the widespread use of machinery in capitalist factories, to conceptualize what workers did in machine terms, and then urge employers to put into practice his "scientific management." First, managers would carefully observe, sometimes with cameras, and time all the movements employees made as they performed their jobs (today, this can be done electronically, without workers knowing they are being watched). In this way, the employer could learn exactly what their hired hands did and how they did it, thereby gaining the knowledge that previously only the workers had. Next, tasks were reconceptualized in machine terms, and a set of exact instructions for each task was developed. Then, those hired would be compelled to perform their tasks in a machine-like fashion, doing just what they were told, that is, when to start, when to rest, how to move, and so forth. All conceptualization of the labor was now monopolized by the employer and his coterie of managers and industrial engineers. Workers simply carried out orders.

In terms of our explication of Marx and Engels's passage, these managerial control mechanisms had two effects upon the workers. First, they significantly deepened the alienation that is implicit in capitalism. The capacity to transform nature through purposive work defines us as a species. In capitalism, this becomes someone else's property. Workers no longer have formal control over it. Before capitalism, most work was relatively skilled, and in early capitalist society, it still was. And since the owners couldn't do it, this gave the artisans some leverage in terms of their production. With the centralization of production, detailed division of labor, machinery, and Taylorism, those who toiled became simply "hands," separated from what they made, from the natural world around them, from themselves. They were now no longer integral human beings but mere sellers of labor power.

Second, and with some irony, the alienation capital creates tends to make labor a homogeneous mass. Workers begin to see themselves in one another inside the factory—all of them wage laborers under the thumb of capital. The detailed division of labor and machinery reinforces their sense of similarity, all as interchangeable parts, or as Marx put it, "appendages" to the machines. As the process of homogenization spreads, as alienation becomes more evident, and as capitalism creates ever more wage workers, a working class is created. All societies come to be divided into capitalist and working classes. Sooner or later, those who toil begin to grasp both that their options are limited and that their lives are circumscribed by the fact that they are considered by their employer as costs of production to be ruthlessly kept within strict limits—often at a level that does not allow for anything but a marginal existence. Likely, they will be wage workers until they are too old or crippled physically and mentally to be hired. Their skills, their dreams, their obvious ability to do other things are permanently stifled. Can they become capitalists? Unlikely. Can they become independent artisans? Hardly. Can they obtain a plot of land and become successful farmers? Doubtful. Inside this system, their prospects are dim.

Out of these realizations the germ of an idea takes hold. As individuals, workers are powerless. But because they are so large in number and their employers dependent on their labor, if they were to come together in solidarity, they could challenge the control to which they are subjected. At first, they rebel in seemingly spontaneous ways, although in any attempts to secure justice and disrupt production there are always leaders and forethought. When, for example, the price of some necessity like bread rose above what were historically fixed or "just" prices, they rioted (in Great Britain in 1795, for example[7]), taking bread from bakeries and destroying the property of their "betters."[8] Sailors sometimes rampaged against their impressment, that is, their capture and compulsory labor on ships. In London in 1780, "the polyglot working class of London liberated the prisons amid the greatest municipal insurrection of the eighteenth century."[9] In the early nineteenth century, the famous Luddite rebellion of English weavers and textile workers shook the government itself.[10] And one of the most critical elements in the making of capitalism, namely slaves, who were surely workers though unpaid and not even nominally free, rebelled in multiple ways throughout the seventeenth, eighteenth, and nineteenth centuries.

As capitalism began to conquer the world and displace prior modes of production, workers became used to it, in the sense that it came to seem "normal" and unlikely to succumb to immediate destruction. However, when the system was young, before, say, the middle of the nineteenth century, people felt the new system as a shock, the complete destruction of their previous ways of living. British historian E. P. Thompson laid out their grievances:

> The rise of a master-class without traditional authority or obligations: the growing distance between master and man: the transparency of the exploitation at the source of their new wealth and power: the loss of status and above all of independence for the worker, his reduction to total dependence on the master's instruments of production: the partiality of the law: the disruption of the traditional family economy: the discipline, monotony, hours and conditions of work: loss of leisure and amenities: the reduction of the man to the status of an "instrument."[11]

Multiply these many times, and we have an idea of how slaves suffered. No doubt the jolt, the blow that capitalism delivered, helps to explain the rage and violence that accompanied the initial working-class uprisings. Even today, when hurts mount and can no longer be endured, similar insurrections occur. However, as time passed, workers became habituated to the capitalist work regimen, and as they realized that prior ways of living could not be recovered, they began to develop more permanent organizations, capable of resisting capital on a long-term basis. The two nearly universal institutions they formed are labor unions and labor political parties.

I will have much more to say about these two working-class formations, but it is important here to understand that many unions and parties originally had a strong anti-capitalist focus. The resolutions and reports of the International Workingmen's Association (1864–1874), in which Karl Marx was the dominant voice, are filled with examples of the exploitation of workers, the need for worker-managed cooperatives in production, the assumption that the ultimate aim of the working class is its full emancipation, and the necessity to support workers in every country. It is either stated directly or implied that complete freedom for workers cannot be achieved within capitalism; it will only happen with its abolition and replacement with a commonwealth of associated producers.[12]

The Industrial Workers of the World (IWW) was more forceful still, with the preamble to its constitution stating:

> The working class and the employing class have nothing in common. There can be no peace so long as hunger and want are found among millions of the working people, and the few, who make up the employing class, have all the good things of life.
>
> Between these two classes a struggle must go on until the workers of the world organize as a class, take possession of the means of production, abolish the wage system, and live in harmony with the Earth.[13]

Even the conservative American Federation of Labor, in its founding constitution, said:

> Whereas, a struggle is going on in all the nations of the civilized world, between the oppressors and the oppressed of all countries, a struggle between the capitalist and the laborer, which grows in intensity from year to year, will work disastrous results to the toiling millions, if they are not combined for mutual protection and benefit.[14]

While individual unions typically have not been explicitly anti-capitalist, socialists have often been among their founders and leaders. Unions have also been key elements in social revolutions, for example, in Russia and Cuba.[15]

When workers develop enough consciousness to grasp their collective power, they naturally want things to change in their workplaces. Whether their efforts are uprisings like those of the Luddites or the formation of labor unions, what they always seek is improvements in their current conditions of employment. We can call their demands defensive, in the sense that they are combating something an employer has done. They seek limitations on the length of the workday or reductions in it, higher wages, safer working conditions, and so forth. When they see that their brothers and sisters in other countries face similar circumstances, they do what they can to support them. They are "proletarians of all countries."

Soon enough, though, workers grasp that their unions cannot always affect matters outside their places of employment. A ten-hour or eight-hour limit on the workday for all who labor cannot be won by a single union. The same is true for constraints on child labor or the outlawing of dangerous substances in all factories. Unions cannot easily prevent wars, slavery, or colonial plunder. These matters are national and international in scope. Capitalism has always come into full flower under the aegis of a national state, which provides for the sanctity of commercial contracts, law and order, a military, and a national treasury that raises money through taxation and borrowing and spends the money necessary to pay for whatever functions it chooses to serve. In those countries allowing voting, workers began to agitate for their right to cast ballots, a right almost always denied them. Where there was no voting, they demanded that there be elections. And in all cases, they began to insist that the state serve their needs. To formalize their political presence, they created political organizations, most prominently working-class political parties. If these could gain control of the government, either by electoral means or armed insurgency, then they could dictate what the state did.

Yet, workers were not ignorant of the political power of capital, so it became clear to some proletarians and their allies among intellectuals like Marx and Engels that political efforts had to be tied to the transformation of both the state and the system of production and distribution. Which meant that they conceived the ever-growing working class as the agent of the ultimate abolition of itself, the ending of class society, and the building of a world of associated producers, ending the multiple alienations of a class society. The proletarians of all countries must unite, with this emblazoned on their battle flags: "From each according to his ability, to each according to his needs!"[16] They have nothing to lose but their chains.

Barriers to Class Unity

While the above discussion of the final lines of the *Communist Manifesto* has a satisfying logic, there is a high level of abstraction implicit in it. Marx and Engels were aware of this, and they wrote about aspects of the concrete reality of capitalist society that were impediments to the class consciousness and radical actions of the working class. There were as well matters they failed to consider. Let us look at a variety of obstacles that impede the class consciousness and unity of the working class. Some of these were examined in the last chapter, but they bear repeating.

The control mechanisms employed by capital open new possibilities for wage workers to develop consciousness of themselves as a class and not simply as abused individuals. Nevertheless, they also are profoundly alienating, and estrangement does not necessarily give rise to coherent thinking. The detailed division of labor, the machinery that deepens it, and Taylorism's de-skilling of labor, make work a monotonous, brain-numbing endeavor. Adam Smith, in *The Wealth of Nations*, extolled the virtues of the division of labor, but he also wrote this:

> In the progress of the division of labour, the employment of the far greater part of those who live by labour, that is, of the great body of the people, comes to be confined to a few very simple operations, frequently to one or two. But the understandings of the greater part of men are necessarily formed by their ordinary employments. The man whose whole life is spent in performing a few simple operations, of which the effects are perhaps

always the same, or very nearly the same, has no occasion to exert his understanding or to exercise his invention in finding out expedients for removing difficulties which never occur. He naturally loses, therefore, the habit of such exertion, and generally becomes as stupid and ignorant as it is possible for a human creature to become. The torpor of his mind renders him not only incapable of relishing or bearing a part in any rational conversation, but of conceiving any generous, noble, or tender sentiment, and consequently of forming any just judgment concerning many of even the ordinary duties of private life.[17]

This is somewhat extreme and may reflect Smith's own class biases. But consider how autoworker Ben Hamper described a visit to the factory, made with his family when he was a boy, to see what his dad did:

We stood there for forty minutes or so, a miniature lifetime, and the pattern never changed. Car, windshield. Car, windshield. Drudgery piled atop drudgery. Cigarette to cigarette. Decades rolling through the rafters, bones turning to dust, stubborn clocks gagging down flesh, another windshield, another cigarette, wars blinking on and off, thunderstorms muttering the alphabet, crows on power lines asleep or dead, that mechanical octopus squirming against nothing, nothing, nothingness.[18]

The problem is that capitalism tends to create the workforce it needs. It must have control, and so the institutions that comprise the system—the market, the schools, the bourgeois scholars, especially the economists, whose work justifies whatever capital does, the ideology of individualism that buttresses the entire edifice—bring forth workers who are compliant. Another way to put this is to say that over time, once the generations whose life worlds were turned upside down by the new society have disappeared, those who sell their labor power come to see it as normal, something they have no choice but to do. The normality extends to the power their bosses have over them. As their humanity is diminished and they cannot exhibit their innate capacity to conceptualize and execute complex tasks, they naturally internalize this as the way things are. When the praises of capital are incessantly sung, it is but a short step to the feeling that if you are not "successful," it must be your fault. You made poor choices, and now you must suffer the consequences.

Beyond the debilitating impact of alienation on working-class struggle, there are, despite the homogeneity that managerial control produces, multiple differences among workers that militate against solidarity. Here are important examples, some of which were touched on above.

Skill. In any business, the skill levels of employees differ, sometimes considerably, and often these variations are associated with other differences. Artisans, masters of a craft, were typically the first wage workers to form labor unions. They had many advantages over the unskilled. They were more likely to be literate; they were more difficult to replace; they were typically homogeneous by gender, race, and ethnicity. In early factories, the less skilled toilers were women and children, frequently orphans farmed out by orphanages to capitalists.[19] Children could hardly resist their exploitation, though the skilled workers could agitate for the abolition of child labor. With respect to women, the patriarchy that has marked capitalism from its inception made it unlikely that men would show solidarity with female workers, especially considering that today men still resent women's employment in many workplaces and make life unpleasant for them. Later, in factories where modern machinery had yet to be introduced, skilled workers employed unskilled helpers.[20] In the United States, the former were usually from northern Europe, and the latter were Irish or from the southern and eastern parts of Europe. Language barriers and the ethnic and cultural biases of English and German craftsmen, as well as their economic incentive to pay the unskilled as low a wage as possible, made solidarity unlikely. The labor unions of skilled workers did not admit the unskilled as members, and federations of craft unions did not offer charters to unions of the unskilled.

Making matters more complicated is the fact that capitalism is an extraordinarily dynamic system. Firms fail, and employees lose their jobs. New firms enter the fray. Old occupations die, and new ones are born. Both changes make working-class organizations fragile. For example, the trade of machinist required a knowledge of engineering drawings, a mastery of geometry, and a delicate physical touch. The workers used their skills to build a strong union. However, after the Second World War, numerical control technology, developed by the Air Force at public expense, destroyed the craft. What the machinists knew is now embedded in computer programs, which operate the machines that convert engineering drawings into machine parts. This has greatly reduced the power on the job of the machinists, who now no longer need a multiyear apprenticeship to perform their work effectively.[21]

Capital Mobility. Capital is mobile both within nations and globally. In the United States, during the three decades after the end of the Second World War, manufacturing was concentrated in the Northeast, Midwest, and Northwest. Labor strongholds existed in many cities and towns, in terms of economic and political muscle. Today, this power has dissipated or disappeared as corporations moved their operations south and southwest where labor was weak. And they began a rapid shift of production to the Global South, in pursuit of low wages and supportive political climates.[22] The same phenomenon is present in all the rich capitalist countries. With this has come a considerable attenuation of political influence at all levels of government, resulting in a loss of the social welfare gains that raised the living standards of workers and made them less vulnerable to the ravages of unemployment, disability, and poor health.

Nationalism and Imperialism. Capitalism developed within the womb of the nation-state, aiding and abetting capital, which, as Marx said, "comes dripping from head to foot, from every pore, with blood and dirt."[23] While state repression has been a critical factor impeding both the birth and the growth of radical labor movements, so too has been the promotion of nationalism, the idea that every person in a country is privileged somehow to be in it, and that it is the duty of all to pledge allegiance to their government. There are circumstances in which nationalism can be a progressive force, such as in anti-colonial and anti-imperial efforts. In general, however, it is antithetical to global labor solidarity. This is because it signals an exclusiveness that makes those from other countries suspect, as I noted in another context:

> Nationalism as an ideology of exclusiveness quickly became very powerful. The establishment of official languages, the institution of a universal propaganda mechanism in the public schools, and the drafting of working people into national armies all had the effect of encouraging workers to be loyal to the nation. The converse of this loyalty has been distrust or even hatred of those who are "foreign." My father was a union-factory laborer for forty-four years, but his life experiences were not conducive to international solidarity. The Second World War, especially, shaped him into an almost fanatical supporter of the U.S. government (and de facto supporter of U.S. capital in most respects) and into an outright xenophobe when it came to the Japanese or the Soviets or the Chinese.[24]

The sway of nationalism in the Global North is evident whenever a nation goes to war. Immediately, most people and organizations give knee-jerk support, including the labor unions. Flag-waving, pledges of allegiance, the singing of national anthems at sporting events give ample evidence to this power. When the First World War began, the Social Democratic Party of Germany, heir to Marx and Engels' International Workingmen's Association, had its elected officials in the German legislature vote in favor of financing the nation's entry into the war. Even erstwhile socialists have succumbed to the lure of nationalism.

Nationalism in the rich capitalist countries is intimately connected to imperialism, the use of state power to dominate the Global South, and, in the process, generate enormous money flows from the dominated to the dominant nations. England, Germany, and the United States have concocted all manner of rationales for their pillage. Racist arguments were used, suggesting that the workers and peasants of the Global South could not develop their own lands and were fortunate that the rich countries helped them do so. The amounts of money extracted from the Global South were large enough that workers in the imperial nations could be co-opted with some of it and be convinced that imperialism was a good thing. It has not been uncommon for labor unions and labor political parties in the rich countries to support imperial wars and their employers' foreign despoliations.[25]

Race and Gender. Modern scholars of the origins of capitalism, following in the footsteps of writers like W. E. B. Du Bois, have argued persuasively that racism and patriarchy are not peripheral to capitalism, in the sense that it is possible to imagine a non-racist and non-sexist capitalism. Rather, both have been integral to the capitalist system, essential for its functioning, then and now.[26] For example, slavery was integral to capitalism, and in the United States, by the late seventeenth century, this was a racial slavery.[27] A deep and complex web of racist ideology came with racialized slavery, so that a "white" race was, in effect, created, superior to the "black" race. So much was this so that it became part of everyone's lived reality. That is, even though biology tells us that there is no such thing as race, this fact is overcome by our identification as white, black, brown, and so forth. We act accordingly, and our societies are structured racially:

> We make individual choices about all sorts of things, we, at the same time, make "social choices." These structure the larger

society, which, in turn, conditions our individual decisions. Our political system is a case in point. The United States was founded as a nation whose prosperity depended heavily upon slavery, which was the dominant mode of production in the southern states and tightly integrated into northern capitalism. The slave trade, the production of important commodities such as cotton and tobacco, the textile industry, shipping, construction, the manufacture of agricultural implements, and many other economic activities were intimately tied to slavery.

The slave economy was supported by a constellation of laws that maintained the entire oppressive system. Who enacted these laws? That is, were the "social choices" that allowed, defended, and maintained slavery made by everyone equally or were the choices of some weighted more heavily than those of others? It would take someone . . . obtuse . . . to argue that in 1789 there was political equality in the United States. Slaves had no political power, and even among those who were not slaves, women could not vote, and, in many states, whites had to own property to cast a ballot. Blacks in the North were nominally free but subject to extreme race and class discrimination. So politics was dominated by white, male property owners, who shaped the government decisively to serve their interests, including the institution of slavery. And by the time slavery ended, inequalities of income and wealth had developed to the point that this white, male, economically elite power was thoroughly entrenched and difficult to unseat. So what this elite wrought was also hard to change. Slavery ended, but the institutional setting in which it flourished did not.[28]

The same argument can be made about patriarchy. Capitalism took the patriarchy that already existed and shaped it to suit the needs of capital.

A racial and patriarchal capitalism generated fundamental splits in the working class, and these have been among the most critical impediments to class unity. Objectively, a working class exists, but this does not mean that its members are conscious of their capacity to disrupt production and the system itself. However, once the importance of race and gender is realized—along with capitalism's third pillar, imperialism—then the way is cleared for the possibility of building a cohesive and radical working class. But this is easier said than done.

Divide and Rule. Capital's representatives quickly grasped the need for and their power to divide workers into hostile and competing parts. Skill, nationality, race, gender—all have been used to split the working class, both in production and what we will call capitalism's hidden abodes.[29] Businesses have gone so far as to structure workplaces with artificial hierarchies, that is, those with no direct connection to productive efficiency, simply to divide their employees into contending groups.[30]

Health. To employers, workers are nothing more than costs of production, to be controlled and minimized. This has profound implications for how employees will be treated. Marx puts the matter forcefully:

> On leaving this sphere of simple circulation or of exchange of commodities, which furnishes the "Free-trader Vulgaris" with his views and ideas, and with the standard by which he judges a society based on capital and wages, we think we can perceive a change in the physiognomy of our dramatis personae. He, who before was the money-owner, now strides in front as capitalist; the possessor of labour-power follows as his labourer. The one with an air of importance, smirking, intent on business; the other, timid and holding back, like one who is bringing his own hide to market and has nothing to expect but—a hiding.[31]

The hiding takes the form of an assault on the body and mind of the laborer, relentless and unending. Throughout the history of capitalism and in every country, most workers have been and are rendered at least partially incapacitated after a lifetime of toil. Specific examples will be given later in this book, but suffice it to say that the health of the working class does nothing positive in terms of its changing the world.[32]

QUESTIONS AND UNCERTAINTIES

From here, we delve into the meat of the matters at hand. How much has the working class changed the world so far? Can it go further and bring about a global transition in which capitalism is superseded by a radically democratic socialist mode of production, with maximum substantive equality across as many social outcomes as possible? Such a society would be one where Marx's dictum, from each according to ability, to each according to need, becomes reality.[33] From what I have written up to this point, we can only say that there are forces at work within the capitalist social order that move workers in this direction. Yet there are others that counteract them. Therefore, the answer to the question depends on which has the greater weight. This is not simply a matter that can be settled by observation of the objective conditions. The two contending classes, capital and labor, have agency—each can act to further its ends. At the same time, the past weighs heavily on each, limiting not only what we can achieve but what we can know with clarity. Not everything will be possible at any given time. First, we must grasp the nature of the world in which we live. Second, we must work out a plan of action to change our circumstances. Third, we must act. And fourth, as we act, we must see what happens, how we are affected, how our comprehension of things changes consequent on our activities, and how our possibilities have been altered. Each step is complex, and we can never be certain of our perceptions, much less the success of our endeavors.

4—What Hath the Working Class Wrought?

I n 2016, workers in India organized a massive general strike. Estimates of the number of participants went as high as 180 million, which would make it the largest such strike in history. All but one of the major Central Trade Union Organisations called for and supported the strike. However, most workers in India do not belong to labor unions, nor are most covered by the country's weakly enforced labor laws. Unorganized employees, many in informal and contracted-out employment, took an active part in the strike. Workers in every Indian state, in all sectors—agriculture, mining, transportation, manufacturing, services, government— and in nearly every occupation, walked out in large numbers. Tens of millions of women struck.[1]

The general strike, one of seventeen that have occurred in India since 1991, should be seen in the context of the twenty-seven years of a government-capitalist alliance that has wreaked havoc on India's workers. State properties have been sold to private businesses; the needs of capital have taken precedence over those of workers and peasants to an unprecedented degree; rural lands have been stolen and privatized; unions and left-wing political parties have been subjected to great state repression; workers have been squeezed to work more intensively, meaning that while productivity rose, employment did not; wages have stagnated; food consumption in the countryside, home to more than 800 million people, has fallen; the oppression of women continues; and ecological crises loom menacingly over the country. Given the difficulties of waging struggles in individual workplaces, rage has boiled over, providing fertile grounds for short general strikes as the best available means of protest.

The main organizers of the strike put forward a list of demands, similar to those in the previous general strikes:

- Contain price rises through a universal public distribution system [see below for explanation] and ban speculative trade on the commodity markets.
- Institute concrete measures for employment generation.
- Enforce all labor laws and stringently sanction violations.
- Provide universal social security coverage for all workers.
- Assure minimum wages not less than Rs 18,000 [about $267] per month.
- Assure pensions not less than Rs 3,000 [about $44.50] per month for entire working population.
- Stop disinvestment of central and state public sector undertakings.
- Stop contract work [precarious work] . . . and institute equal wages for same work.
- Require registration of unions within a period of 45 days and immediate ratification of ILO [International Labour Organization] conventions C87 and C98 [these guarantee the rights of people to free association and to organize for mutual protection, including bargaining collectively with employers].
- Stop labor law amendments [restricting workers' rights].
- Stop FDI [foreign direct investment] in railways, insurance and defense.[2]

These are worthy demands. They address the conditions of the entire working class and not just those of a particular group within it. The first demand is especially noteworthy. The Indian government has established a network of Fair Price Shops, which sell basic foodstuffs to the poor in publicly-owned shops at subsidized prices. This "public distribution system," which began in 1947, has left much to be desired in terms of coverage, corruption, and quality of the goods sold. The unions' request doesn't address these problems, but it does insist on universal coverage. That is, every Indian would have access to the shops, something that could help alleviate the country's food crisis.[3] To keep prices low, the demand includes a curb on commodity speculation, which has been responsible for spikes in food prices.

The fact that so many Indians embraced the demands and stopped work throughout the nation is remarkable, as is the great diversity by class, caste, gender. industry, and occupation of the strikers. Nothing remotely similar could take place in today's United States, or in any rich capitalist country.

And yet, except for some increases in the legal minimum wage, India's working class has little to show for their spectacular general strikes. The conditions of the class continue to deteriorate. The country is now led by a neo-fascist, Narendra Modi, a man not inclined to be sympathetic to the needs of workers. His party, Bharatiya Janata, promotes an extreme form of Hindu nationalism, and in February 2002, when Modi was chief minister of the Indian state of Gujarat, he fanned the flames of an orgy of anti-Muslim violence, including rapes, that claimed some 2,000 lives. Afterward, Modi said that he "felt the same pain over the bloodshed as a passenger in a car that has just run over a puppy." He referred to the refugee camps set up to shelter some of the 200,000 Muslims who lost their homes as "baby-making factories." And his minister for women is now serving 28 years in prison for murder and conspiracy to murder.[4] To Modi and his government, the plight of workers and peasants is of little concern. Repression, on the other hand, is a pillar of the state's reaction to all working-class and peasant struggles that threaten capital.

The Working Class Has Changed the World

The depredations of capital are legion, relentless and pervasive, forced upon us with fierce intensity and violence. No assault on humanity, no annihilation of nature will be forgone if money can be made. *Theft* is capital's watchword. And yet, from capitalism's birth centuries ago, those harmed most by its imperatives have resisted. Their defeats have been many, their victories too few. However, their struggles have changed the world. Peasants have resisted with their own organized violence the expropriation of their farms and common lands. Wage workers, including those unemployed, have marched, picketed, boycotted, struck, sat-in, sabotaged, stole and destroyed their employers' materials, and petitioned governments. They have contested capital's power in every institution of their societies, from schools to media to religion. There have been times when both peasants and workers have engaged in armed battle with both capitalists and governments. In a few cases, alliances of workers and peasants made revolutions—in Russia, China, Cuba, Vietnam. Women were critical in all these alliances.

Slaves were in a constant state of revolt throughout the period of modern slavery. Escapes, destruction of equipment, theft, and violence occurred—with slaves all the while maintaining a collective solidarity that, in retrospect, is astonishing. What is more, slaves engineered the first successful anticolonial revolution, freeing Haiti from French rule and slavery in a long war between 1791 and 1804. This sent shock waves throughout the Caribbean, the United States, and Europe. Slave owners and governments feared that the spirit of revolt would spread, which it did.[5]

WHILE MARX AND ENGELS URGED the proletarians of the world to unite, efforts by workers to change their world have been overwhelmingly confined to the countries in which they live. This, as noted in chapters 2 and 3, was due to the solidification of the nation-state and the power of nationalism that this engendered. The two forms that these struggles took have been labor unions and working-class political parties and agitations. Let's look at each in turn.

Labor Unions. Unions are a universal response of the working class to capital's oppression. Labor movements show considerable differences across countries, but they also exhibit several similarities. For our purposes, the parallels are most important, and what can be said with certainty is that unions dramatically change the conditions workers face inside their places of employment and, to some degree, in society itself. Not only do they win higher wages, benefits such as healthcare and pensions, and improved working conditions, unions also weaken the control employers have over hiring, promotion, layoffs, discipline, the introduction of machinery, the pace of work, and plant closings.

An examination of the impact of unions in the United States is useful. Union density—the fraction of the employed who are in unions—is lower there than in almost any country in the Global North. In 2017, it was 10.7 percent.[6] The average for the thirty-four relatively rich capitalist countries in the Organisation for Economic Co-operation and Development (OECD) is 17 percent. However, in the Scandinavian nations, densities are greater than 50 percent, with Sweden, Finland, and Denmark at about 65 percent, and Iceland at a remarkable 92 percent.[7] The lower this density, the weaker the union impact on wages, benefits, and wage inequality.[8] Therefore, if unions in the United States positively affect the lives of working people, then it is reasonable to conclude that they have done the same in the other countries in the Global North and very probably in many nations in the Global South as well.

Statistical analyses show clearly that unions raise wages above what they would otherwise be. If a researcher took a large sample of wage earners and noted for each worker in the sample the wage

rate and as many variables as economic theory predicts should
influence the wage rate, such as years of schooling, age, occupation, geographical location, marital status, experience, health,
and attachment to the labor force, along with union membership, he or she could isolate the impact of union membership
on the wage rate. That is, a technique can be used that in effect
holds all the variables fixed except union membership. In every
such study, the union wage premium is positive, often highly so.
In the United States, using 2011 data, this premium was 13.6
percent; union workers earned 13.6 percent higher wages than
similarly situated non-union employees. There are significant
variations around this average. The union advantage is higher for
black, Hispanic, Asian, and immigrant workers, which, because
these groups have lower wages on average than do white workers, lowers the racial/ethnic gap in pay. For the same reason, this
reduces overall wage inequality. Furthermore, unions benefit
most those in the lowest-paying occupations and industries, as
well as those with fewer years of formal schooling, again reducing inequality.[9] While the union premium for women is smaller
than that for men, union power does increase wages for women
in the female-dominated service sector; here they are higher for
union women than for their sisters in non-union service sector
work.[10] A remarkable achievement of unions is that they have
taken low-wage labor and revolutionized pay scales. Before U.S.
workers rose up collectively during the Great Depression of
the 1930s, automobile, steel, rubber, electrical, dock, mine, and
packinghouse workers suffered subsistence wages and deadly
working conditions. Workers were industrial serfs. Their unions
forced employers to remunerate them at levels unimaginable
before their revolt. From the mid-1960s to the early 1980s, uprisings among California's farm workers, led by the United Farm
Workers, brought wages that most people would not believe.
Historian and former farm laborer Frank Bardacke points out
that lettuce piece-rate workers, doing highly skilled work in
teams of three, were earning in the early 1970s, thanks to their

militant strikes, a wage as high as $10 per hour.[11] This is equivalent to a wage of more than $60 an hour today.

Unions also exert a threat effect. Non-union employers might find it expedient to raise the wages of their employees if they want to avoid unionization. Or they might be compelled to pay more to secure an adequate supply of labor power. Whatever the reason, non-union wages are higher when unions are strong than when they are not. It is even possible for union wages at a particularly large employer to force other local employers to raise wages. An example is the hospitality industry in Orlando, Florida: "Negotiations between six local affiliates of the Services Trade Council Union (STCU) and Disney World in 2014 led to wage increases for union members to at least $10 an hour starting in 2016. These local affiliates represent housekeepers, lifeguards, cast members, and other service workers. Disney then extended the raises to all its 70,000 Orlando employees, including non-union employees. According to the *Orlando Sentinel*, the wage increases prompted much of Orlando's hospitality and retail sector, including Westgate Resorts, to raise wages."[12]

Unionization brought with it benefits that only salaried managerial personnel had enjoyed. Chief among these are healthcare, pensions, and paid time off. In the United States, in the early 2000s, 83.5 percent of union workers were covered by healthcare insurance, and 71.9 percent had pension coverage, compared to 62 percent and 43.8 percent respectively for non-union employees. The union premium for healthcare was 28.2 percent and for pensions it was 53.9 percent. Unions brought a 26.6 percent advantage in terms of vacation weeks. Retirees have profited from their union workplaces, not only because they collect better pensions but also because, for many of them, their employer-financed healthcare carries over into retirement. The union premium here was 24.4 percent.[13]

Many types of work are deleterious to physical and mental health. Unions have been paramount in forcing employers to provide safe workplaces, free of injury and health hazards. Collective bargaining agreements typically contain detailed health and safety clauses.

Workers are aware of these, and they will enforce them through both a grievance procedure and, when necessary, by direct actions such as refusals to perform unsafe work or strikes. Union employers are better informed than their non-union counterparts about health and safety laws, and their unions know how to get these statutes enforced. In especially dangerous work sites, such as construction projects and coal mines, the union advantage can hardly be overstated. "In 2014, OSHA [Occupational Safety and Health Administration] inspected New York State construction sites and found twice as many health and safety violations at non-union construction sites as at union construction sites. Another study, of Missouri construction sites, found higher levels of OSHA violations among non-union St. Louis residential construction job sites than at unionized St. Louis residential job sites."[14] "Unionization is associated with a substantial and statistically significant drop in traumatic injuries and in fatalities in underground bituminous coal mines from 1993 to 2010."[15]

The mental stress of jobs often gets overlooked. People are expected to buck up under any strain and carry on with their work. Yet we ignore employment trauma at our peril, as regular incidents of violence, including murder, by disgruntled employees prove. Imagine the impact of the tragedy of 9/11 in New York City on first responders, especially firefighters. The poisons in the air those days has crippled and killed many of them, generating enormous pressures on their families too. Individual unions have worked hard to do something about these matters:

> Firefighters who develop PTSD after witnessing repeated trauma on the job don't always have recourse if the disorder means they cannot work while they seek treatment. When independent studies showed that post-traumatic stress rates are on the rise for Texas firefighters, the Texas State Association of Fire Fighters (TSAFF) launched an education campaign for state lawmakers leading to legislation to improve workers' compensation coverage for Texas first responders diagnosed with

line-of-duty-related PTSD. The legislation (HB 1983) was signed into law by Governor Greg Abbott on June 1, 2017.[16]

Three critical functions of labor unions are that they give workers a voice on the job, guarantee due process, and educate their members about a wide variety of important subjects. In non-union workplaces, capital has untrammeled power, unless there are laws prohibiting certain conduct. Without laws, capital can hire and fire "at will" in the United States, meaning, for example, that workers can be hired, fired, demoted, or reassigned for any reason, or no reason. You can be discharged because your boss doesn't like your politics or the color of your hair. Your wages can be arbitrarily cut, and your benefits rescinded. These things can happen in union environments, but they can be challenged, again through a formal grievance process or direct worker action. The grievance system creates due process procedures that must be followed, and these usually end in some form of binding arbitration in which a neutral third party investigates what happened and makes a ruling. If union workers are especially strong and militant, they often take immediate action, such as an unauthorized strike, slowdown, or sit-down to rectify the wrongs management has done. Automobile worker Gregg Shotwell gives readers an excellent example of direct action, used to challenge the authority of a foreman:

> I hired into GM [General Motors] and joined the UAW [United Auto Workers] in 1979. I didn't know much about how unions worked. I soon learned. At six-thirty one morning, we were sitting around sipping coffee and trying to wake up to a new day of the same old shit. A foreman who was new to the area told us to get up and get to work. "Right now," he said. "I'm the boss." We said, "Yes sir, boss." We went right to work. Thirty minutes later, every machine in the department was down. Then skilled trades came out, tore the machines apart, left parts all over the floor, and went off to look for the missing parts. They didn't come back. There was no production that day. Every department behind us

went down like a domino. The next morning, the same foreman said, "Good morning, gentlemen." Then he left us alone to do our jobs.[17]

I have had personal experience as a labor arbitrator, and on more than one occasion I reinstated a fired employee, with full backpay, after determining that the company had wrongfully discharged him. Every year, unions win thousands of arbitrations, something that non-union workers cannot take advantage of. Some non-union businesses have employee handbooks, which spell out certain employee rights, often including the right to file a grievance. But almost always, the company reserves for itself the final say.

Unions can, if they are robust enough to do so, win input into such managerial functions as hiring, introducing new technologies, relocating a plant, or even closing an operation or an entire facility. At the least, a union can compel an employer to pay for the right to do what it wants. Some unions, especially in construction and on the docks, have hiring halls, so that when a company seeks to hire new workers, it must get them through the union-administered hiring hall. For example, workers who loaded and unloaded cargoes from ships were once hired through a "shape-up," in which those who wanted employment showed up at a gate, and a boss would select whomever he wanted for a particular job. This method was open to the grossest forms of bias and extortion. When the stevedores unionized, they demanded an end to the shape-up. The employer must now request a work crew from the union, and the union must send the senior unemployed workers to the job site. Employers can be made to give workers notice and severance pay for plant closures, as well as the right to transfer to another corporate facility. They might win early retirement rights if they are of a certain minimum age. When new technology is introduced, union workers might enjoy the right to be taught how to operate new equipment. Or they might be paid a wage, out of a special fund negotiated by the union and the employer, whether they labor or not when mechanization puts them out of work.

Businesses can be forced to pay worker retraining costs, including education expenses.[18] With respect to mechanization, when a new production technique is put in place, employers will usually try to enforce new output standards. Industrial engineers will monitor workers, nowadays with sophisticated equipment that might not entail the direct scrutinizing of those operating the new machinery. They will decide what the new quota should be, that is, how many units of output or task repetitions a typical worker should produce or do during a specified time. To counter this, organized workers might agree among themselves to sabotage the engineer's efforts by slowing down. However, this won't work if they don't know when or even how they are being watched. The union might then insist on its own engineer to at least provide a more worker-friendly and less intensive estimate of what a worker might reasonably be expected to do.

In some European nations, mainly those with high union densities, union voice has penetrated deeply into what would normally be considered arbitrary management rights, that is, the rights implied by capital's ownership of the constant capital. Union voice in Europe is examined below, but two examples of labor's power there are worth noting. Recall that in chapter 3, mechanization as managerial power was illustrated with the example of numerically-controlled machines. These helped to destroy the craft of machinist by taking the knowledge of this skilled artisan and embedding it electronically in a tape, which was then attached to a tool that would automatically convert a block of metal into a machine part specified in an engineering drawing. In the United States, operating a numerically-controlled machine requires training, but nothing like that demanded of a true machinist. A few weeks does the trick, and then the worker is monitoring a piece of equipment, not doing something that requires great skill. There is no reason why former machinists, or newly hired workers, could not learn to write and edit the programs that operate the machines, just as machinists once worked with the engineers who made the original drawings of what a machine part should look like. However, employers couldn't imagine giving workers that kind of autonomy. In Norway and other Scandinavian countries, metal workers' unions insisted on empowering their members:

> The possibilities of worker control can be seen from a look at the "trade union participation project" of the Norwegian Iron and Metal Workers Union at the government-owned weapons factory in Kongsberg. The Kongsberg plant recently introduced the latest type of NC machines, Computerized Numerical Control (CNC). CNC machines come with a built-in mini-computer, made feasible by the introduction of micro-processors. These computer units allow info from a number of tapes to be stored in the machine and allow editing and changes in the tapes right on the shop floor. If a machine operated by tape has to be corrected by the manual intervention of the machinists—as is often the case—the computer automatically "corrects" the tape for future use, and on some models programs for complicated contours on metal parts can be made right at the machine on a keyboard console. This new technology makes it possible for workers on the shop floor to regain control over the work. The machine operators could not only edit tapes but make their own programs from scratch.

> However, this potential hasn't yet been realized here in the USA. At the big General Electric plant in Lynn, Massachusetts, for example, the computers on the new CNC machines remain locked and only management is allowed to edit tapes. Managers simply don't want the workers to gain more control over the operation.

> But at the Kongsberg plant the machinists normally do all of the editing of the programs, according to their own ideas of safety, efficiency, quality and convenience. They add or subtract operations, or alter the whole sequence, to suit themselves. All of the machine operators are trained in programming, and there is

a cooperative spirit between the programmers and the machinists. As one programmer said: "The operator knows best; he's the one who has to actually make the part and is more intimately familiar with the particular safety and convenience factors; also he usually knows best how to optimize the program for his machine." This situation came about, not because Kongsberg has a more "enlightened" management, but because as the fruit of a struggle waged by the union.

When the Iron and Metal Workers Union was first faced with the problem of new computer-based technology, they hired a computer outfit, without collaboration with management, to do research for them. After explaining the new technology to some of the unionists, a number of pamphlets were produced, written by and for shop stewards, and a new position was set up in the union—the "data shop steward." The data steward is responsible for keeping up with technical developments and looking over all new management proposals with a critical eye. Another union person is also assigned to keep an eye on the data steward, to make sure he doesn't become too much of a "technical man," that is, out of touch with rank-and-file feelings.[19]

The Ford Motor Company introduced the concept of producing a product along a series of interconnected machines, an assembly line, which it implemented in 1913. Most other high-volume manufacturers followed suit. The advantage for capital was that it pushed managerial control of the labor process to a new level. Workers were now indeed "appendages" to the machine. It is difficult for those of us who have never worked a line to imagine the sense of alienation and stress such labor engendered. Here is how an employee at a Subaru-Isuzu plant in Indiana described what she had to do in about forty-five seconds. To save space, I have skipped many of the steps:

1. Go to the car and take the token card off a wire on the front of the car. 2. Pick up the 2 VIN (vehicle identification number)

plates from the embosser and check the plates to see that they
have the same number. 3. Insert the token card into the token
card reader. 4. While waiting for the computer output, break
down the key kit for the car by pulling the 3 lock cylinders and
the lock code from the bag. 5. Copy the vehicle control number
and color number onto the appearance check sheet. . . . 8. Lift
the hood and put the hood jig in place so it will hold the hood
open while installing the hood stay. . . . 22. Rivet the large VIN
plate to the left-hand center pillar. 23. Begin with step one on
the next car.[20]

It is possible to imagine a reconceptualization in which production teams learned every aspect of car, truck, or bus production,
working with engineers and then making the products collectively
without an assembly line. This is what Volvo and the automobile
workers' union did at a plant in Uddevalla, Sweden. Teams of
employees performed a variety of tasks in pre-assembly stations,
and then the partly assembled cars were moved by conveying
devices to be finally assembled, again by work groups. Alienation
fell, and productivity rose.[21]

The formation of a union is a collective effort, and engaging in it,
confronting the boss, is bound to make workers think about what
they have done and what they hope to achieve. That is, labor unions
are bound to raise the consciousness of those who form them. At
the same time, labor organizers always try to educate prospective
members, and the union itself provides educational materials and
may even have developed more formal educational programs for
the rank and file. The best unions insist that new members learn
the history of the union, the provisions of the relevant labor laws,
the political platform of the union, and the details of bargaining
and filing grievances. They might have special meetings, short
courses, and longer schooling opportunities for the rank and file.
Good unions also work hard to involve members in every facet
of union work. Active participation in grievances, strikes, picketing, boycotting, and political agitation helps to further strengthen

working-class consciousness, making workers stronger in their convictions and willing to live the precept that an injury to one is an injury to all. A working-class way of looking at the world begins to take shape, and this prepares workers for whatever struggles ensue during their lives. Labor education programs, now usually attached to colleges and universities, provide education for members. Special courses can be constructed for individual unions, or classes of a more general nature can be offered. Workers can sometimes earn college credits and degrees in such programs. Through such education, workers can deepen their understanding of work, power, and organization, and this can also help them to develop class consciousness, a grasp of the nature of the society in which they live and are exploited and alienated.[22]

Another important change that unions bring to the workplace is dignity. Unions oblige employers to treat their employees not as "hands" but as human beings. The fact that the leaders of the rank and file sit across the bargaining table from their bosses as equals means a great deal to workers. It was not uncommon for those who built the great industrial unions in the United States during the Great Depression to say that they joined the unions not so much for material gains but for what unions meant to their psyches, to their sense of worth, to their need for respect. Coal miners once had to go home after their shifts underground covered with dust and grime. The United Mine Workers demanded that bathhouses be constructed at the job site, so that miners could return home clean, looking like those who claimed to be their "betters." In a society built upon enormously unequal power and daily exploitation, respect becomes more critical than we might think.

Labor Politics. By their nature, labor unions are defensive organizations, aimed mainly at their own members' working conditions. They must wage war against the employers who hire those they represent. But they don't do battle with all employers. They may be able to win the support of other unions and workers, even to the extent of a general strike, such as those that took place in

India, noted at the beginning of this chapter. However, whatever unions may do, sooner or later they must confront government. The state, at every level, is intertwined with capital, labor's primary adversary. Governments purchase goods and services from corporations. They collect taxes and spend money. The largest and most powerful states have virtually unlimited taxing and spending power. Governments make and enforce laws; they have the only legitimate (in the sense of being formally legal) police power. The courts ultimately determine the meaning of the laws. Important components of government regulate a wide array of activities and groups of workers that might concern business, such as those in public health, housing, infrastructure, transportation, workplace safety, and care for the elderly, the poor, the unemployed. The state has the power to regulate and influence financial markets; its actions here can pressure interest rates up or down and make it harder or easier to borrow money. States wage war. No matter what the government does, capital exerts its economic power to limit tax liabilities and receive as much public spending as possible, to influence the selection of judges, or to counter anything that challenges its social power. Given all of this, unions have little choice but to be politically engaged.

Unions have embraced a range of political programs and philosophies. Typically, they have united in federations or national organizations, which then operate in the political sphere on behalf of member unions and often in the interest of all workers. These have sometimes been crucial to the founding of labor-centered political parties, although some national groups simply allied themselves with already existing parties.

In the United States, the first craft unions (carpenters and other building trades workers, cigar makers, iron molders, machinists, and other skilled laborers) joined together in 1886 to form an umbrella organization, the American Federation of Labor (AFL). Its president, Samuel Gompers, espoused what has been called "bread and butter" unionism, which urged unions to focus on winning higher wages, shorter hours, and better working conditions, and to eschew politics. By the 1930s, this philosophy had hardened into a posture that saw government intervention in workplace matters as an absolute evil. Whatever security workers needed could be won through organizing and negotiating with employers. The AFL even opposed federally-financed unemployment benefits, at a time when there were record numbers of people out of work and on bread lines. The AFL seemed to believe that if workers were given money by the state, they wouldn't see a need for unions.

The AFL stance was always hypocritical. First, it opposed the unionization of the less-skilled workers who were coming to dominate the labor force in the large industrial factories that were now central to the economy. Not only did the craft unions disparage the unskilled, they were racist and patriarchal, often viciously so. The AFL didn't mind supporting the government when it entered the folly of the First World War, and it then helped the state in its persecution of the radical Industrial Workers of the World (IWW), whose members were opposed to the war and its carnage, the victims of which were overwhelmingly working class. Second, the craft unions in the AFL functioned mainly at local levels. Here they always did political work, given that local governments spent money on construction projects, roads, streetcar lines, and the like, which always required skilled labor. The craft locals wanted this work, and to get it, they often had to get in bed with local politicians. In strikes, police at both local and state levels might be called to arrest strikers, and courts might issue injunctions. Political connections were obviously needed, and the unions sought them out.

During the Great Depression, the U.S. labor movement came alive. The Communist Party, born after the Bolshevik Revolution of 1917, had tried to build its own unions, but these had limited success. However, the Party had many experienced members and allies in heavy industry, most notably automobiles. Communists began to organize the unemployed as well, and they were successful in anti-eviction campaigns and mass rallies for government relief. In the mid-1930s, working-class agitations began to develop in mass-production industries, and under the leadership of United

Mine Workers (UMW) president John L. Lewis, a new national labor federation, the Congress of Industrial Organization, was born. The CIO soon took in new unions, and some old ones affiliated with it. While the organizing drives, picketing, and sit-down strikes that engulfed heavy industry were often led by Communists and other radicals, the CIO soon established strong ties with the Democratic Party. These have remained intact ever since. In 1955, the CIO and the AFL merged to form the AFL-CIO. This occurred after a post–Second World War wave of anti-Communist hysteria had succeeded in getting the CIO to purge its left-led unions. After this, the AFL-CIO continued to be a faithful ally of the Democratic Party, contributing large sums of money to Party candidates for political office and actively campaigning for Democrats at all levels of government.[23]

The CIO and the AFL-CIO have championed pro-labor laws that benefit not just union members but the entire working class. The CIO actively supported the enforcement of the National Labor Relations Act (NLRA) of 1935. This law was enacted shortly before the CIO began, but it was sharply attacked by capital and its conservative allies in the U.S. Congress. The AFL also was hostile to the new statute, arguing that the National Labor Relations Board (NLRB), charged with interpreting the act and assessing penalties for violations, favored CIO unions. CIO lobbyists courted help from potential allies in Congress to give teeth to the NLRA and NLRB. The labor federation gave its support to the passage of social security legislation and a wage and hours law. After the Second World War, the AFL-CIO pushed for enactment of the Occupational Safety and Health Act and the various civil rights acts. Today, union lobbyists are busy in every state capital and large city. The recent "Fight for $15" movement, which seeks to win at least a $15 minimum wage and has organized short strikes of fast-food workers, is supported strongly by the AFL-CIO and several member unions.[24]

Around the world, some working-class entities opposed active involvement in what we might call bourgeois politics. In the

United States, the IWW was the best example.[25] Its philosophy, which is named syndicalism, contends that workers, organized in democratic unions, can gain control of the means of production through extensive strikes, culminating in general work stoppages. Both during and after such strikes, workers will themselves manage collectively society's productive wealth. Syndicalism was most popular in Italy, France, and Spain in the early decades of the twentieth century. Closely related to syndicalism is anarchism, a political philosophy and practice that is much alive in the world today. The Occupy Wall Street movement that commenced in 2011 and many of the recent struggles against the rise of fascism have been spearheaded by anarchists.[26]

More common than either the pressure-group strategy of the AFL-CIO or the syndicalist position of workplace-centered anticapitalism has been the formation of labor political parties. These either form along with labor unions and federations or after unions have achieved some economic power. It is not uncommon for union and party membership to go together. In Europe, such parties have existed since the mid-1800s, and they have achieved considerable success in advancing the interests of the working class. Great Britain provides a good example.

By the middle of the nineteenth century, unions had been established, mainly among skilled workers. In 1868, organized workers formed a central labor federation, the Trades Union Council (TUC), which is organized much like the AFL-CIO. As Britain's only major labor federation, most unions are members of the TUC. Unlike the AFL-CIO, it did not align itself with one of the major mainstream political parties, the Liberals or the Tories. The growth of a militant union movement, including the organization of unskilled workers, during the late 1880s gave rise to the formation of a working-class political party. Historian Wolfgang Abendroth gives us some of the history:

With the founding of the Independent Labor Party (ILP), 1893 saw the embryo of a mass labor party. Its ideology was derived largely from Christian socialist and democratic traditions, and it marked the beginning of the first systematic independent political activity undertaken by large sections of the working class . . . . In 1894 almost a quarter of the delegates to the Trades Union Congress were members of the ILP, and the ILP began to penetrate the TUC's parliamentary committee, hitherto the lynchpin between the unions and the Liberal Party. Although this development often met with obstruction . . . a resolution in favor of supporting working-class parties was tabled successfully at the TUC in 1898. On 27 February 1900, the first conference of the Labor Representation Committee was held and called for an independent workers' party.[27]

The Labour Party immediately attracted large numbers of working-class votes, winning thirty seats in the 1906 elections. It succeeded at times in entering coalition governments and forming majorities between 1906 and the end of the Second World War, but it never pushed forward a strong working-class perspective. Labor's leaders actively supported Great Britain's entry into the First World War and gave tepid support for the ill-fated General Strike of 1926. However, the Labour Party came into its own after the Second World War. British capital's parties, reeling from the war's devastation and extremely unpopular for their lukewarm opposition to fascism before the war, were soundly defeated, and the Labour Party took command of the government. It introduced Keynesian taxing and spending programs, nationalized certain industries like coal and steel, and created a modern welfare state, including the National Health Service. The NHS is run directly by the government, is free, and includes a wide array of services to everyone. This was a tremendous achievement, and it removed one of the most important insecurities from working-class life. The Labour Party, with the backing of the unions closest to it, gave social welfare benefits full legal status. Whereas in the United States health insurance is typically dependent on employment and is paid for in full or, more likely, in part, by the employer, in Great Britain it is mandated by law and free to the recipients. Workers in Great Britain also enjoy 5–6 weeks of paid vacation, again written into law.[28]

If we look at other European nations, except for those that were once part of the Soviet bloc, we see much the same trajectory, but with differences of degree. Where union density is high and labor political parties have had long periods running governments, social welfare benefits tend to be the most generous and comprehensive. In Sweden, for example, the Social Democratic Party (SAP for its Swedish initials, literally Social Democratic Workers' Party of Sweden), which was allied with the Swedish Trade Union Confederation (usually known as the LO, its Swedish initials), held decisive political power for more than fifty years, beginning in the mid-1930s. Most of Sweden's labor unions were in the LO, and many members were also in the SAP. The LO negotiated national agreements with a confederation of Swedish employers, while the SAP constructed a system of benefits that became the envy of the world. In return for union wage restraint and to allay the burden of high progressive taxes—levied to help employers compete in world markets in an export-driven economy—the state socialized large swathes of consumption. Here is a partial list. Note that, while not included in this list, college education is also free for European Union citizens.

Health and Sickness

1. Subsidized doctor care, mainly in county clinics
2. Free public hospital treatment
3. Subsidized dental care; free for children
4. Subsidized prescription drugs; lifesaving drugs free
5. Free abortions and sterilizations
6. Free maternity clinics for prenatal care
7. Cash benefits to compensate for loss of wages due to illness; separate benefits available for workers injured on the job

Family Support

8. Tax-free monthly payment to parents for each child; single parents receive an additional payment for each child
9. Parents can take a total of 12 month's paid leave at near full wages to care for each child up to first year in school
10. Subsidized childcare at home or in a government day-care center
11. Childcare for one year at a subsidized nursery school
12. Unemployment insurance of about 80 percent of previous income

Pensions

13. Three different kinds of old-age pensions, paid for by taxes and employer contributions
14. Full or partial disability pensions; disabled child pension goes to parents until child is 16 and then directly to child
15. Special payment to handicapped persons who are working or in school
16. Surviving spouse and orphan pensions

Additional aid is provided only to those who have low incomes. The most important is the housing subsidies for poor families and elderly pensioners.[29] The other Scandinavian countries have similar social welfare programs.

In Germany, unions were politically sophisticated from the beginning. In 1875 the German Social Democratic Party was formed as a merger of two earlier working-class parties. It is still in existence and has held national power frequently. As with the rest of the rich European countries, it was after the Second World War that a well-developed social welfare system took hold. Besides many benefits, workers also have access to exceptional vocational training. The content of the training is overseen by government, employers, and unions, and workers have a decent opportunity to secure work that utilizes their training. These highly skilled workers produce high-quality goods that help to guarantee the success of German exporters.

The German system is "corporatist," which means that labor and capital are seen as social partners, and the state is intimately entwined in their relationship. German labor law, for example, is much more encompassing than that of the United States and Great Britain. Detailed laws regulate collective bargaining, guarantee all workers certain benefits, prohibit unjust dismissal, and dictate union participation in all national commissions, agencies, and policy-making bodies having to do with labor-related matters. There is also a system of codetermination, through which workers can, indirectly, through their unions, participate in corporate decision making, including "the appointment of the management board members, monitoring of business operations overseeing the activities of the management board and, in a subcommittee, determining the compensation of its members. With the supervisory board approving major strategic decisions, ultimate corporate power resides with it and thus also with employee representatives."[30]

At the firm level, there are works councils, open to all workers, union and non-union alike. The councils have a wide range of powers. The councils and employers decide hours, safety and health, job classifications, and dismissals, among others. A decision on these cannot be taken unless the council agrees. The councils also have the right to know firm economic information, and they have the right to consult with the employer before new technologies can be introduced. Collective bargaining agreements are negotiated at the industry or corporate level, but the councils watch over their implementation. They can also bargain local agreements.

In Germany and every European Union country, employees can only be fired for cause, which means that it is much more difficult to discharge workers. They will either have access to binding arbitration or the courts. There is no such thing as the at-will employment that plagues most U.S. workers.

Outside of the rich capitalist countries, there are labor-based political parties, and, of course, there are labor unions. Several of India's dozen or so labor union federations are affiliated with national political parties. Unions can bargain with employers, especially in industries in which the government is the main employer and in private sectors such as automobiles and textiles. Political agitations and nationwide strikes have compelled governments to enact protective legislation similar, at least in form, to those in the countries of the Global North. Throughout the Global South, however, serious constraints keep workers from achieving what some in the Global North have won. Protective laws are either absent or weakly enforced. Many states stand ready to violently suppress the working class and have frequently done so. This is not to say that there are no rich nations in which similar problems exist; the United States readily comes to mind. But for reasons that will become clear in the next chapter, there is now little chance that European-style social welfare benefits will be coming to the world's poorer nations. In Iran, for example, there have been many labor uprisings, with strikes and demonstrations, all of which have been illegal under Iranian law. The protesters demand unpaid wages in a climate of runaway inflation, political corruption, endless wars, and staggering inequality. They have been ruthlessly suppressed by the government. The state authorities sometimes back off and make concessions, but the price paid by the working class is high. Beatings by thugs paid by the authorities, mass arrests, imprisonment, and torture are not uncommon. That the workers continue to rebel is a testament to their courage.[31]

Another difficulty facing the working classes in the Global South is the precarity and extreme difficulty of working-class life. A high proportion of employment is in the informal sector, done in the home or small workplaces, with much work contracted, and often re-contracted out. In India, for example, there are more than five million *bidi* workers. They hand-roll cheap cigarettes and small cigars (*bidis*), in their homes or in workplaces notorious for miserable conditions. The pay can be as low as $1 per day for twelve hours of labor. More than 90 percent of *bidi* laborers are women, in a society that is extremely patriarchal. In such circumstances, it is difficult to form labor unions or engage in political action.[32]

There are union and union-like organizations among informal-sector workers. Waste pickers in Brazil, minibus drivers in Georgia (the country), *bidi* workers in India, street vendors in Liberia, and domestic laborers in Uruguay have all formed organizations, gaining laws to protect themselves and engaging in negotiations with both state and private entities to improve their economic conditions and strengthen their rights. A domestic workers' union, the Sindicato Unico de Trabajadoras Domésticas (SUTD), was formed in Uruguay in 1985. It didn't have much success under military governments but came to life when democracy returned in 2004. It helped to get protective legislation enacted, with the new law granting domestics the same labor rights as other workers and establishing a wage council. The council consists of three members from government, two from the SUTD, and two from a league of employers of domestic workers. Negotiations have taken place over the past decade, and agreements have been reached, after contentious discussions. Wages have increased considerably, and a fund has been set up, with contributions from employers, so that the women who did union work could be paid while they were performing it. Members of the SUTD continue to do household labor for their employers even if they also have union duties.[33]

Labor and Revolution. There has been no social revolutions, in the sense of an overthrow of capitalism, in any rich socialist nation, but there have been several in the Global South. The first took place in Russia in 1917. While the working class, concentrated in the larger cities, was relatively small, it was militant, weary from wartime slaughter, food shortages, and corruption. Strikes and demonstrations were widespread. Workers and the much larger peasantry formed numerous soviets (democratic councils) that began to take matters of production, distribution, and protection into their own hands. Historian Tamás Krausz provides a telling description of the situation in October 1917 and shows that, while the First World War was the catalytic agent, the Revolution was driven forward by the working class and peasants:

> By October, 20 million people had organized in the soviets, but even earlier, in the summer of 1917, the soviets had a membership of 9–10 million people. The revolution was driven by the social self-organization of these millions of tortured people disillusioned by the war—especially in the workers and peasant soviets [councils in towns, factories, etc.], military and revolutionary committees, factory and plant committees, the professional and armed self-defense organizations. All were loosely structured for people's mobilization, production, land distribution, and wielding of power, and all accomplished through a great deal of spontaneity and invention. The land decree accepted at the Second All-Russia Congress of Soviets was also such an original product. It simultaneously expressed the desire of the peasants for land, and for social equality. The land was delivered to the peasants by way of an initial nationalization, so that it could not be bought and sold, and thus was removed from the sphere of market conditions and capital accumulation: "The land belongs to those who work it."[34]

The Revolution was successful, in that the Bolsheviks managed to consolidate state power. However, this was only after years of civil war, aided and abetted in the most brutal manner by the imperial powers, mainly Great Britain and the United States. The soviets were not able to consolidate their own nascent power and build a working-class society, especially after Stalin gained absolute power. Great gains were still made for the workers and peasants of Russia, and after the Second World War for the countries in the Soviet bloc. Guaranteed employment, excellent education and healthcare, run by the state and free of charge, subsidized rent and food, exceptional art, literature, music, and science, and a considerable erosion of patriarchy are some of the Revolution's major achievements, not to mention its primary responsibility for the defeat of the Nazis in the Second World War.

We can say much the same of the socialist revolutions in China, Vietnam, and Cuba. The first two countries were overwhelmingly peasant societies, so rural people made up the core of the forces who fought for and won revolutionary victory. Consequently, land distribution and, in China, the eventual consolidation of small holdings into large-scale peasant communes, which not only were able to feed their members but provide food for those in China's many large cities, were central to what happened after these revolutions. In both countries, great improvements were made in schooling, health, and overall social welfare for the masses of people. In Cuba, there was a proportionately larger working class than in Russia, China, and Vietnam, and workers helped Fidel Castro and his armed force gain power in 1959. Since then, tremendous advances in the lives of the Cuban people have been made. Education, healthcare, and, today, organic farming, urban agriculture, and medical research are world class. Progress against racism, patriarchy, and homophobia have been remarkable.[35]

A signal achievement of the working class and peasantry in the Global South, both in those countries that made socialist revolutions and those that did not, is the assault they made upon colonialism and imperialism. Before substantive changes could occur in the lives of the masses of people, the control wielded by colonial powers had to be broken and imperialism had to at least be weakened. Workers and peasants did this throughout the impoverished nations of the world.

It is fair to say that, from the beginning of capitalism, workers and peasants have fought capital. They came to see that this system would never, on its own, accord them a better life. Quite the contrary, it would drive them to further misery. Struggles against their class enemy have resulted in tremendous and positive changes in the lives of the oppressed and expropriated. If we think about what life was like for nearly all workers when modern capitalism first exploded in Europe, these improvements can only be described as monumental. The same can be said for Chinese peasants before and after the 1949 Revolution. And yet, workers and peasants are nowhere close to their full liberation, in the sense meant in this book.

To this point in the chapter, I have focused on what the working class has achieved in its struggle against exploitation, the first aspect of capitalist oppression. With respect to the second element of this subjugation, expropriation, labor unions and political organizations have done some good. Most unions and political parties are committed to racial, ethnic, and gender equality. It is common for collective bargaining agreements to contain broad no-discrimination clauses. Some are committed as well to affirmative action, so that, for example, the race, ethnic, and gender composition of union leadership mirrors the share of these groups in the larger population. During the Great Depression in the United States, the Packinghouse Workers union not only organized black meatpackers but actively helped to integrate working-class neighborhoods, including restaurants and bars. Some unions strongly supported the civil rights movement.[36] A few unions, notably those with majority women membership, have female presidents, and both women and minorities now have greater access to better-paying jobs than was once the case. The gap between the wages of women and men is lower in the rich European countries than in the United States, and this can be largely attributed to the demands coming from the labor movement and worker-centered political parties.[37] The expropriation of nature will be further discussed in chapter 6, but here we can say that the labor movement in the Global North has done very little to oppose the theft of peasant lands in the Global South. In their own countries, Northern labor has championed policies and programs, as well as collective bargaining provisions, that make workplaces healthier spaces and countries less polluted.[38]

5—The Power of Capital Is Still Intact

I n 1980, the world population was 4.45 billion. Of this, the number of people in the USSR and China was 1.25 billion, 28 percent of the total. More than a quarter of the world lived in countries that had broken out of the capitalist global market. In these two countries, production was not predicated on profit, employment was guaranteed, and much of consumption by workers and peasants had been socialized, that is, provided without payment by individuals. In China, immediately after the victory of Mao's Red Army in 1949, land was distributed to tens of millions of peasants, satisfying one of the Revolution's major slogans, "Land to the Tiller."[1] Gradually, the Chinese Communist Party urged peasants to begin to pool resources and work collectively. The culmination of this process was the establishment of communes throughout the Chinese countryside. What followed were gains in production, the development of local technological initiates, and the empowerment of the peasantry. Predating the communes, but progressing much further, was the spread of rural education and health, controlled by the communes and giving rural people things that had been inconceivable. Collective self-sufficiency and security were the goals, and to a considerable extent, these were achieved.[2]

THE SOCIALIST BLOC INCREASED THE POWER OF WORKERS AND PEASANTS

The emergence of two socialist behemoths placed a brake on U.S. imperialism, which then, as now, is the most dangerous anti-working-class force in the world. The Soviet's decisive role in defeating fascism in the Second World War made the communists who led the resistance popular in most of Europe. Communist parties were poised for electoral success in Greece and Italy, and the Communist Party in France wielded great influence within the French working class. The intelligence agencies of Great Britain and the United States worked overtime, employing murderous methods and misinformation campaigns, to prevent communist victories, but workers still held members in high esteem. We will see shortly what this meant for wage workers.

In the Global South, the Soviet Union and then China provided models for radicals seeking fundamental social change. Both countries, for various and not altogether altruistic reasons, gave support, both ideological and material, for anti-colonial and anti-imperial struggles. The Chinese army intervened in the Korean War, sending troops into battle, and forcing the United States to end its genocidal onslaught against the North Koreans. The Soviets aided the Vietnamese revolutionaries in their war against another U.S. genocide. The Soviets also supported the Cuban Revolution and many other revolutionary struggles, including the anti-apartheid movement in South Africa and anti-imperial efforts in Latin America. The fact that the United States and the other nuclear powers in the Global North faced a highly industrialized adversary with its own nuclear weapons forced a different political calculus to be made by these countries than might otherwise have prevailed. Both the working class and the peasantry throughout the world were given some breathing space for any opposition they mustered against capital.

In both the Global South and Global North, the presence of a significant socialist world—which came to include many other

countries besides China and the USSR—compelled the imperial states to moderate their collaboration with capital in its war
against laborer and peasant. Without a global communist movement, it is doubtful that India's government would have pursued
a left-of-center development trajectory, one that avoided the
total penetration of its economy by transnational capitalists. The
same applies to the autonomy Mexico sometimes exacted against
U.S. capital, as well as to Indonesia under Sukarno, who led the
independence struggle against the Dutch colonialists. In Africa,
Algeria, Tanzania, and Egypt were able to follow an independent
development program that might not have been possible absent
the communist bloc of nations.

In the Global North, especially in the advanced capitalist economies of Europe, the fear of a left-wing labor movement compelled
capital to recognize and deal with workers affiliated with social
democratic parties and governments. These parties were not radical; they neither foresaw or favored the overthrow of capitalism.
They might appear socialist from the vantage point of the United
States, but that sets a low bar. Their political programs assumed the
indefinite continuation of capitalism and set about creating social
welfare benefits that would make both labor unions stronger and
eliminate the major insecurities of working-class life. In these they
succeeded remarkably well, and from the end of the Second World
War until roughly the 1980s, the working classes of these nations
saw marked improvements in their lives.

By the 1980s, strains in social democracy began to show. Capital
began to chafe at costly regulations, high progressive taxes, and
empowered workers. Low unemployment rates, enforced by government expenditures and public employment, led to wage growth
unacceptable to capital. Many countries had enacted capital controls,
which limited the ability of employers to export capital (in both its
physical and money forms) and take advantage of profit opportunities in the Global South. The last straw in Sweden came with a plan
put forward by economist Rudolf Meidner in 1976 for the Swedish
Trade Union Confederation (LO). The LO proposed that employers

issue new shares of stock to their workers so that in twenty years, the employees would own 52 percent of the firm. Meidner hoped that this would give rise to a peaceful transition to socialism. Swedish employers, supported by the more conservative leaders of the Social Democratic Party, were not amused. They fought against the plan, and it was never implemented. And like their compatriots in the other rich capitalist countries, they joined in more open warfare against labor. Working-class power, buttressed by state welfare spending, was threatening profit margins; global competition was intensifying; and the economic prosperity built upon the pent-up demand after the Second World War was weakening.

NEOLIBERALISM

In response to declining profit margins, capital launched a political project that has come to be known as neoliberalism. Capital's power, reflected not only in ownership of the means of production but also in the pressure it could put upon governments, gradually began to win the war. Its approach was twofold. First, the rich and their allies opened an ideological offensive, financing think tanks and media that bombarded the public with anti-government, anti-labor, and pro-"free market" propaganda. Right-wing economists argued that Keynesian policies didn't work, generating both unemployment and inflation. Protective labor legislation simply priced workers out of the market by artificially inflating wages. Unions were painted as undemocratic dues-collectors that interfered with the workers' freedom to deal with employers individually. Social welfare programs made people dependent and unwilling to work, hurting those the programs were supposed to help. Capital controls, including tariffs and import quotas, hurt the poor in the Global South and promoted inefficiency in home-country industries. Social commentators argued that civil rights legislation, which in the United States helped black workers, was unnecessary, and put minority job applicants in positions their qualifications didn't warrant. The same logic applied to female employees.

Employers began to take bolder actions as this ideological offensive began to bear fruit, in public opinion polls and election results. They now were more willing to ignore labor laws, to confront unions more directly and openly, refusing to negotiate in good faith and sometimes actively courting strikes so they could replace union workers. They introduced draconian control mechanisms in workplaces, using what have been termed "lean production" techniques. These include systematic hiring to avoid appointing union-sympathetic applicants, just-in-time inventories and just-in-time hiring to minimize both labor and material costs, constant speedup of the labor process, closer monitoring of employees with punishment for "slackers," and the grouping of workers into teams responsible for coping with all problems, as well as monitoring and censoring themselves. Workplace propaganda mirrored practices in the larger society. It is now common for employers to call their workers "associates" and "team members," denying in the process the very words that identify the labor side of class composition. Everyone is now alike; capitalists and workers are on the same team; we're all capitalists at heart.

Governments soon began to respond favorably to what employers were doing and what their ideological spokespersons were saying. Judges friendly to the neoliberal project were appointed and they began to make capital-friendly decisions. In the United States, President Ronald Reagan in 1981 summarily fired 11,000 striking air traffic controllers, a draconian measure that dramatically showed just how employer-friendly the national government had become. Over time, a panoply of public policies was effected that gave definition to neoliberalism. The following quote refers to the United States, but much the same could be written about nearly all capitalist societies:

While all of this was taking place, capital began to push for a restructuring of the global economic architecture, using the political power that their money gave them to bend the government to their will. From the 1980s until the present, capital has demanded and gotten an end to public regulation of their businesses and the use of their money. Banking was deregulated, so that financial institutions could make loans, underwrite corporate expansion and mergers, create scores of new, often risky financial instruments, and hold minimal reserves as protections against financial turbulence. Of great importance, governments began to allow the free flow of money and investment across international borders. Trade agreements took from governments the power to regulate foreign investment and finance. The financial sector of the economy grew to become the commanding height of capitalism, accounting for a continuously larger share of total corporate profits. To further weaken the working class, capital pressured governments at all levels to privatize public services. As governments did this, public workers lost employment and the public suffered a marked decline in what they had come to expect from government. Perhaps the most radical privatization has occurred in public education, which has also become a center for the indoctrination of children into the wonders of "free" markets.[3]

Neoliberalism has been the dominant political trajectory in the capitalist world for nearly forty years. For workers and peasants, it has been a disaster. Profits have soared as the wage share in national income has tumbled. Work intensity has sharply increased, and those who labor have found their lives more insecure. Poverty has risen. Public services have shrunk. Union densities have fallen. Governments bend over backwards to satisfy the needs of capital. Inequalities of income and wealth have not been as severe since the 1920s. Ecological crises, long in the making, have been exacerbated by the deregulation of markets and by the extreme luxury consumption of the rich. The theft of peasant lands has become epidemic. Prison populations have climbed rapidly.[4] It is difficult to put in words the misery austerity has caused or to comprehend the callousness with which it has been implemented. Suffice it to say that governments and their corporate backers have committed a very large number of murders and condemned millions of people to lives of hopelessness.

THE COLLAPSE OF THE SOCIALIST BLOC

At the end of the 1980s, the Soviet Union imploded. One reason for this was the failure of the Soviet system to empower workers and peasants. While much of their consumption was subsidized or fully socialized, their work was not. In a system of top-down central planning by a relatively small political elite intent on maintaining its power and privileges, those who produced society's goods and services were mainly seen as cogs in the production machinery. Firm managers were under heavy pressure from the State Planning Committee (Gosplan), whose economic experts constructed the national economic plan, to meet quotas and receive bonuses, so they utilized control mechanisms and techniques like those used in capitalist businesses. Given the near impossibility of firing workers, work effort often diminished, reflecting the alienation arising from being subjected to control without having real power. To get necessary inputs, managers built a system of black markets, and petty forms of corruption became a way of life. A large share of the national budget was devoted to defense expenditures, including those for the disastrous war in Afghanistan, giving rise to shortages of consumer goods, which were often of low quality. People supported one another's petty enterprises to help friends and neighbors earn extra money and to make up for the shortfall of basic commodities. However, this was in opposition to the overall planning process, not as a socialist adjunct to it. The USSR's leaders proved incapable of radically changing direction, and they were not able to keep the system intact.[5]

The breakup of the Soviet Union, followed by the fall of Communist Party control of the Soviet satellite nations in Eastern Europe, had calamitous consequences for the working classes of these nations. In Russia, for example, capitalism was introduced with a vengeance. Party elites and their cronies quickly gained ownership of major firms, including public utilities, in one of the largest and quickest thefts of the people's property in history. Unemployment, unheard of before, reached extremely high levels. Social services disappeared. As production fell, the resulting economic depression caused life expectancies to drop noticeably, an unprecedented event in an advanced industrial nation. Inequality became a fact of life, and today Russia has numerous billionaires. Globally, the now large reserve army of labor in the Soviet countries gave rise to numerous profit opportunities for capital in those places. The exodus of people seeking employment wherever they might find it provided cheap labor in the Global North. Thus, the working classes everywhere were weakened.

One thing that events in the Soviet Union and Soviet bloc countries shows is that years of central planning, socialized consumption, and technological and scientific achievements did little to foster a socialist consciousness, at least among the elite. In China, Mao Zedong understood that it was necessary to focus strong attention on the relations of production, at the same time building a collective economy and a collective consciousness. Capitalist ideas and norms—and in China, feudal—don't die just because capitalism has been overthrown. They live on in mass consciousness, especially that of former elites. Mao had many enemies in the Communist Party, those whom he called "capitalist roaders." He struggled to defeat them, but he failed. After his death, the Party leadership began to make radical changes in the economy. The most significant change was the dismantling of peasant communes, which, though not perfect, had helped peasants improve their life circumstances and to learn cooperative production and develop a communal consciousness. Peasants also lost their social welfare benefits. Since it was not possible to live well on the small plots of land they became owners of after the 1949 Revolution, peasants were forced to move to urban areas where they supplied a large force of cheap, exploitable labor for capitalist enterprises, many of them foreign. Again, the significant increase in the reserve army of labor hurt workers everywhere.

The high growth targets set by the leadership meant suppression of worker and peasant consumption to finance extremely high levels of investment spending. Dam-building, mining, and manufacturing have meant the expropriation of peasant land. The mania for growth has also generated harmful and fatal pollution of air and water. As in the former Soviet Union, inequality rose quickly, with China going from one of the world's most egalitarian nations to one of the least. China, too, has a sizable number of billionaires.

THE DEMISE OF SOCIAL DEMOCRACY

The fall of the Soviet Union and the headlong rush toward capitalism in China gave capital a green light to push back against both unions and social democracy. Capital's offensive has had different trajectories in different places. In countries like the United States, where social welfare benefits were never particularly generous, corporate capital managed to begin the dismantling of what the working class had won by the late 1970s. It was a Democratic president, Bill Clinton, who ended "welfare as we know it" in the 1990s, but this just continued a trend that had begun years before. Social welfare was destroyed abruptly in Eastern Europe. Even in Germany, where the unification of the nation began with the fall of the Berlin Wall in late 1989, those living in the former East Germany have still not managed to catch up with those in what used to be West Germany. Journalist Kate Connolly, reporting from Berlin, said this:

> States in the former west continue to be considerably richer than those in the former east, where ordinary households own far less than half of the wealth accumulated by those in the west. . . .
>
> There are many reasons for the differences, including the fact that wages in the east continue to be lower—at €2,800 (£2,075) a month, people earn about two-thirds of the average wage in the west—and that property in the east is only worth half as much as in the west. . . . The net wealth of the average westerner is about

€153,200 per person. In eastern households it is not even half that. Indeed, East Germans with net assets of at least €110,000 are considered to belong to the richest 10% of adults; in the west, €240,000 is the minimum. As cars are the most conspicuous indication of a German's wealth, it is worth noting that a West German is twice as likely to drive a BMW, with an East German twice as likely to drive a Skoda.

The risk of an East German slipping into poverty is about 25% higher than that of a West German. However, life expectancy has risen considerably in the east since reunification, with women now on a par with their western counterparts. For men, it is slightly lower in the former east.[6]

In Germany as a whole, as in the rest of Europe, cuts in social welfare have already been made or are in the making. Although public financing of social welfare assistance has remained intact, strains are showing. The German government is cutting public investments in order to maintain benefit financing, a sure sign that pressures to cut the social safety net will continue to mount. German capital would rather have better roads, ports, and other infrastructure than pay high taxes to support working-class healthcare.[7] Even the vaunted Scandinavian model, the gold standard in cradle-to-grave security, faces strains and opposition. As in Europe as a whole, union densities have fallen, getting lower since the 1990s. Unemployment rates are higher than historic averages, productivity has fallen off, the ratio of employed to population has fallen. In addition, "The proportion of temporary jobs is high by international standards. In all countries there are signs of new dividing lines, pressure on the lowest wages and growing wage dispersion inequality, deteriorating working environments and increased exclusion in parts of the labour market. These tendencies are reinforced by high labour migration after EU enlargement, which has intensified competition for the lowest-paid jobs and made it harder for groups with low skills or work experience to gain a foothold in the labour market."[8]

In France, the Macron government, which came to power in 2017, is dismantling the country's labor protections in an effort to make the labor market "freer" and more competitive, code words for aiding capital in its war against labor. "In September [2017], Mr. Macron decreed myriad changes, including capping court-ordered fines for dismissals and giving companies greater powers to negotiate working conditions with employees. One part of the broad package is a measure that absolves companies from using lengthy, complex procedures for voluntary layoffs."[9] The *Wall Street Journal* put it this way: "Mr. Macron's agenda mimics in some ways Germany's reforms in the early 2000s under then-Chancellor Gerhard Schröder, who made widespread changes to labor rules and the welfare state, as well as overhauls in the Netherlands and Scandinavia. In all cases, the goal was to protect Europe's cherished 'social model' of capitalism with a strong safety net, while adapting it to the competitive pressures of globalization."[10] Unfortunately, the "social model" and the "competitive pressures of globalization" are not compatible. The first empowers workers, the second weakens them.

Social democracy was badly shaken by the Great Recession that overtook capitalist economies beginning in 2007. Unemployment rose dramatically, poverty increased, and growth rates plummeted, turning negative as the recession hit bottom. Governments everywhere responded not with higher spending, public employment, and progressive taxes, but with austerity. Neoliberalism was still the order of the day. And as is always the case, inequalities that might be masked somewhat by overall economic growth cannot be hidden in a serious downturn. As states embraced austerity, the poorest in each nation suffered most. The most unfortunate were immigrants, whose numbers rose as conditions in the Global South worsened. In Europe, public generosity ended when it came to new arrivals. Among nations, inequalities rose as well. The poorer nations in the European Union became further separated from their rich counterparts. Greece provides the best example. The recession, which was exacerbated by the financial chicanery of German and Greek capital, took an enormous human toll, with people unable to find work and tens of thousands going hungry, unable to pay for food, much less housing and healthcare. Government-imposed austerity measures crippled daily life for millions of Greeks.[11] This was written in 2015:

> Who is affected? Virtually everyone in Greece. Unemployment runs at 25 percent—twice what it was before the austerity program began in 2010—while youth unemployment is at 50 percent. State pensions have been slashed by as much as half, and 30 percent of Greece's population now lives on or below the poverty line, including 40 percent of children. Soup-kitchen lines are filled with former middle-class professionals. In winter, a thick layer of smog hangs over Athens as residents who can't afford heavily-taxed heating oil burn wood to keep warm. Homelessness is rife. The suicide rate has risen by 45 percent. Many young professionals have fled the country altogether; Greece's population—now about 11 million—has fallen by 400,000 in five years. "Our children will grow up in a destroyed country," says Charalabos Nikolaou, a street vendor in Athens. "As prisoners, not citizens."[12]

To deal with the Greek crisis, the richer European nations imposed austerity conditions on bailout loans to Greece, making a bad situation worse.

Social democracy was ascendant, in both its weak U.S. form and its strong European incarnation, during the three or four decades after the end of the Second World War. This was a period in which pent-up demand, high private and public investment to rebuild war-torn countries, Keynesian economic policies of strong government spending and progressive taxation, relatively powerful labor movements, and the existence and example of the socialist bloc generated a widely shared if still unequal prosperity in the Global North. Neoliberalism has put an end to the advance of social democracy. Capital no longer sees a need to accommodate the working class in any way. Money now has the freedom to move with warp speed across the globe, and there is little that any government, with the exception of the United States—whose government doesn't want to anyway—can do to prevent outflows of profits when capital chooses to move its funds from a country that has had the temerity to challenge its power. If, for example, England, France, or Sweden were to try to implement policies that radically empowered workers and unions, capital would surely flow out of the country. The currencies of England and Sweden would come under attack as speculators sold pounds and krona, pushing their price down compared to other monies. This would make imports more expensive and put pressure on central bankers to engage in actions that would raise interest rates, which would then lower both consumption of durable goods and capital investment. New plants would be more likely to open in the Global South than at home.

Years of austerity and attendant belt-tightening have dampened working-class expectations. And constant and continuous ideological propaganda against government has made people distrustful of the state and more willing to accept the magic of the marketplace and their own efforts to improve their condition.

LABOR UNIONS AND POLITICAL ORGANIZATIONS REVISITED

There are two main actors on capitalism's stage, the capitalist class and the working class. Capital is ordinarily the protagonist; it controls the commanding heights of the economy and dominates the political arena. However, labor is not a passive entity. It always has agency, capable of taking actions not only to defend workers but to take the offensive against its antagonist. It is a rare situation in which workers and peasants have no potential power. This means that if we examine contemporary societies, it is fair and necessary to ask what labor unions and political bodies have done to counter neoliberalism. Let's look at each in turn.

Unions. Labor unions have greatly improved many aspects of working-class life, both inside workplaces and in the larger society. Without unions, workers, and peasants too, would be poorer, less healthy, more likely to be injured on the job, have lower life expectancies, be less likely to get an education, and less socially mobile.

However, if we look honestly at most unions, it is remarkable how often they come to resemble in their structure and actions their adversary. They are bureaucratic, with undemocratic chains of command. Their leaders take on many of the trappings—expensive homes and cars, overly large expense accounts, private schools for their children, and the like—of their class enemy. Their radical beginnings have often given way to distrust of the rank-and-file, rampant nationalism, and conservative politics. In the United States, both the AFL and the CIO supported the Cold War, which at home sought to tame an often-militant labor movement, one in which radicals were prominent advocates of civil rights and an end to U.S. imperialism. Globally, it has been an exceptional labor movement that has actively opposed what governments and corporations have been doing in the Global South. Internally, unions have not done nearly enough to combat patriarchy, racism, and homophobia.[13]

Capitalism brings forth the workers it needs, with attitudes shaped by capitalist institutions. It also tends to bring forth the unions it needs as well. The United States provides what may be the most egregious examples. It is a rare national union that elects officers through the direct votes of the membership. The United Auto Workers (UAW), widely hailed for its liberalism, has been called a one-party state, with the Administrative Caucus determining who the leaders will be and autocratically suppressing dissident movements inside the union.[14] Like other unions, the UAW's officers draw high salaries, although with a compensation package of some quarter-million dollars, the UAW president is relatively poor. The Teamsters' president makes nearly $400,000; the Laborers' leader comes in at nearly $700,000; the head of the Carpenters' leader takes in more than $550,000.[15] These salaries are minuscule compared to those of the CEOs of corporations, but they put union officialdom in an economic stratum well above that of the average rank-and-file union member. This level of pay allows for a lifestyle of considerable comfort, as well as nicer homes and better schooling for the children than those afforded ordinary workers. When the leaders face their corporate counterparts across the bargaining table, they might be more likely to identify with them than with those they represent.

When unions are run in a top-down manner, with limited internal democracy, corruption often follows. U.S. unions are notorious for it. Numerous examples could be mentioned. Kickback schemes, theft of union funds, looting of pension plans, and cozy relationships with organized crime are just some of the bad behaviors of those entrusted with the fates of millions of workers. One of labor's best muckraking journalists, Bob Fitch, called the whole sorry business, "Solidarity for Sale."[16] Even the legendary United Farm Workers union, led by Cesar Chávez, has ended up as a set of business hustles run by Chávez family members.[17]

In the advanced capitalist countries, strikes and other militant tactics were necessary to organize workers and compel capital to recognize them. But invariably, once unions have been established, more controlled types of conflict become standard. These are usually sanctioned by laws that mandate collective bargaining and often place legal barriers to strikes, especially walkouts not authorized by union leadership. Given the undemocratic nature of so many unions worldwide, union officialdom has a stake in not allowing the rank and file to exhibit too much initiative and display of working-class power. In this, it shares a bond with employers. The result of this has been a tendency toward establishing cooperative relationships with capital. In return for ceding basic managerial prerogatives to management and for keeping a lid on member combativeness, businesses agree to regular wage and benefit increases.

After the Second World War, the large industrial unions in the United States, led by the UAW, worked out what has been called an "accord" with the dominant big capitalist enterprises, such as the major automobile, steel, and electric companies. Just after the war, the UAW still had many Communists and Party allies in its ranks, including its president. The union demanded that General Motors raise wages without raising prices. For the corporation, such a demand was anathema because it threatened what was integral to generating surplus value, namely control of the business. At the same time, the national government acceded to business demands to modify the National Labor Relations Act. In the 1947 Taft-Hartley Act, capital got what it wanted, with numerous new restrictions on what unions could do to combat the class enemy. One of the provisions of the new law was the demand that union officials at all levels, from national to local, sign an oath that they had no Communist Party affiliations. Almost all unions capitulated to this demand and not only signed the oaths but threw the reds out of them. The CIO eventually purged the left-dominated national unions. In one fell swoop, labor lost its most militant organizers and negotiators and its most anti-racist and anti-imperialist ideologues. The stage was then set for the implementation of the accord. Unions would not challenge managerial prerogatives, and they would keep a lid on member-led actions against their employers.[18]

The accord ushered in an era of labor-management cooperation and a tightening of the bonds between labor and corporate leadership. Labor leaders were now statesmen, looking after the health of the corporations and abandoning mass strikes for the good of the country. UAW dissident Gregg Shotwell puts the matter bluntly in describing former UAW president Ron Gettelfinger:

> Gettelfinger is a corporatist: that is, he believes our fortunes as union members are tied to the company's apron strings. At the Ford sub-council, where union members convened to devise a bargaining strategy, he invited Lord Ford and his stooges to explain how sacrifices would be necessary. Ford's problems are not the fault of union members or union wages. Does Ford invite UAW members to Board of Directors meetings to advise

them how they should make sacrifices for the good of the community?[19]

The answer to Shotwell's question is, No. Corporations never countenance worker interference with their assumed right to unilaterally determine how their property will be utilized. They might accept, under the duress of class struggle, a tactical retreat that allows some union participation in decision making. However, they will always chafe at such interference with their managerial "rights," and they will find ways to circumvent it.

Union autocracy, corruption, and the accord together meant that when capital discarded the accord in the 1970s and embraced neoliberalism, the unions were unprepared. Labor had pretty much abandoned organizing the unorganized, making a business-like calculation that the costs outweighed the gains. The organizing that still existed failed to use the tried-and-true method of massive face-to-face meetings and home visits with workers and the active involvement of the rank and file in every facet of the organizing campaign. And the examples of cooperation and complacency, lack of democracy, and leadership chicanery gave employers easy anti-union propaganda opportunities. Then, as corporations began to close plants and cut their workforces to become lean and more profitable, unions failed to respond actively and with full member participation. Each plant was in competition with every other worksite, making cascading concessions to employers inevitable. Union density began to plummet in the 1980s and has continued to fall since. Meanwhile, the unions continued to urge employers to return to the accord. The results, by any measure, have been disastrous.[20] In a startling display of labor-management collaboration, the president of the New York State Building & Construction Trades Council, an umbrella organization comprised of the major construction unions in the state, co-authored a newspaper editorial with the CEO of a major business group condemning efforts to provide universal health insurance in New York. Too bad if many residents in a major state have inferior insurance. The union members have great plans. Solidarity with the rest of the working class? Forget about it.[21]

Although corruption has been less problematic in the European labor movement, it is hardly nonexistent. A union-run bank in Austria is a case in point:

> The recent collapse of the union-controlled bank BAWAG (Bank für Arbeit und Wirtschaft) in Austria, however, would certainly qualify as an example of fundamental union corruption comparable to or surpassing American labor corruption. One German commentator described the scandal as "the downfall of the Austrian worker's movement." The BAWAG, the fourth-largest bank in Austria, engaged in speculative business dealings in the Caribbean, which resulted in the loss of approximately 1 billion euros. The Austrian Labor Federation (ÖGB) oversaw the bank, and the running shopping list of inept and criminal activities of the ÖGB could be attributed to a union leadership who were more interested in a wannabe-capitalist banker lifestyle rather than protecting the assets of ordinary rank-and-file members. The ÖGB turned the BAWAG into a criminal enterprise. The illegal practices of the BAWAG have resulted in the loss of the strike fund, an education fund for the children of union members, and an emergency assistance program for members who are experiencing a financial crisis. Union expenditures in Europe are not as transparent as in the United States. Consequently, union corruption in Germany is simply better disguised and therefore unregistered by many American labor journalists and commentators.[22]

Labor-management cooperation, however, is more common, especially in Germany, where, as we saw in chapter 4, the industrial relations system is corporatist. Union leadership is as divorced from the rank and file as in most U.S. unions. The same model, with variations, is widespread in Europe, and for much the same reasons as in the United States, the main exception being the greater fear of a communist-led movement in Europe. Norwegian labor activist and union official Asbjørn Wahl is worth quoting at length, because he lives in one of the richest European countries, Norway, a nation with a high union density and perhaps the best example for the achievements of social democracy. Wahl is skeptical that there can be a renaissance of welfare capitalism, that is, a return to the heyday of social democracy.

> Unfortunately, mobilizing working-class power is not the project of the trade union movement in Europe today. The paradox labor faces is that while the economic and political climate in which the trade unions must operate has changed enormously, most unions have continued to pursue the policy of the social pact. They consider so-called globalization to be not the result of conscious strategies and new power and class relations, but rather the necessary consequences of technological and organizational changes, a position remarkably similar to that expressed by Margaret Thatcher when she infamously said, "There is no alternative." What is needed, they say, is to transfer the policy of the social pact from the national to the regional and global level. Their methods are "social dialogue" with employer organizations and state and suprastate institutions, campaigns for the formal introduction of labor standards (such as the labor conventions of the International Labour Organization [ILO], which, among other things, prohibit forced labor, guarantee the rights of free association and collective bargaining, and prohibit employment discrimination) in international trade agreements and trade organizations, as well as the pursuit of corporate social responsibility (CSR) codes of conduct and framework agreements with multinational companies. These latter are voluntary, unbinding, and unenforceable codes of conduct developed by the multinational companies themselves. So far, they have had no identifiable effect on corporate behavior and seem to have as their main aim counteracting the negative public image of many multinational companies.[23]

The results have been similar to those in the United States. Unions have proven unable to reverse the impact of neoliberalism, and workers have continued to face falling union densities, stagnating wages and benefits, cuts in social welfare benefits, and rising inequality. Fortunately for European labor, the wage and benefit base is much higher than in the United States, and the higher union density has allowed labor to prevent the wholesale destruction of the welfare state. For now, at least.

With respect to the hidden realms of capitalism, those that involve expropriation, some unions have done better than others in combating racism and patriarchy. Yet there are many examples of unions treating minority and female members in a discriminatory manner. In the United States, craft unions once refused to accept African Americans as members (they were barred from admission by the unions' constitutions), and racial disparities still plague unions in terms of holding union office and access to jobs. Women are woefully underrepresented as union officers.[24] European unions do better, but they still exhibit both racism and patriarchy, especially in their treatment of recently arrived immigrants.[25]

Labor and Politics. What has been said about labor unions is equally true for labor's political entities. Again, the United States gives us the most extreme example. Organized labor has tied itself to the Democratic Party, which by no stretch of the imagination can be described as a labor party. It has, in fact, abandoned whatever concern it had for working people, believing instead that a coalition of highly educated suburbanites and traditionally Democratic minorities gives it the only chance to gain state power. Yet, despite this, the AFL-CIO and most of the member unions contribute tens of millions of dollars and untold hours of phone-banking, house calls, and social media work to get Democrats elected, no matter how conservative these politicians are. In 2011, for example, Richard Trumka, AFL-CIO president, and James Hoffa, Jr., head of the Teamsters union, were sharply critical of then-president Barack Obama and the Democratic Party for catering to business and ignoring the working class. Forget for a moment that these labor leaders have been far removed from the working class for a very long time, and Hoffa, who is an attorney, never did a union job like those his members do every day. Their reproaches were well founded. Yet, when Obama ran for a second term, they were all-in with the rank and file's money and time. Hillary Clinton, who, if anything, was even more pro-capital than Obama, got the endorsement of Trumka and nearly all AFL-CIO unions. The unions shunned Bernie Sanders, a left-liberal who actively courted those who do society's work. The Democratic Party treated him like a pariah, whose candidacy was wrecking it. Clinton tried to tar him as pro–Fidel Castro, when, to his credit, he refused to denounce Cuba during a debate. An independent labor politics rooted in militant action is as far removed from the thinking of U.S. labor chiefs as can be imagined. They will do anything to maintain a mythical seat at power's table, seemingly oblivious of the truth that no one at that table sees them sitting there.[26]

In Great Britain, the Labour Party long ago abandoned its commitment to the working class. Under former prime minister Tony Blair, the Labour Party embarked upon a "third way" politics, supposedly trying to occupy a position between the evils of right and left, one that again relied upon an educated professional and technical class attuned to the demands of the modern world. In practice, what this meant was continuous compromises with the right and the distancing of the party elite from the labor unions. Somehow concessions to the right—in other words, capital— would bring something good to the masses. Unfortunately, capital always wants maximum exploitation and expropriations. To capitalists, conciliation is a temporary phenomenon, and sooner or later, they will claw back whatever they have conceded and restore the "free market." Margaret Thatcher wasn't kidding when she said, "There is no alternative" to the war of all against all that is the essence of capitalism. She saw this war as a good thing, because a ruthless leader like herself would survive unscathed. It is difficult to believe that Blair and company did not believe the same, given their adherence to neoliberalism when they led government. This became clearer still when they reacted with horror when a man considerably to the left of Bernie Sanders, Jeremy Corbyn, was elected to head the Labour Party. One would have thought that Vladimir Lenin had just been chosen.[27]

In the stronger social democratic parties, the trends are the same, moving steadily rightward, harming the working classes of their respective countries in an effort to ward off attacks from conservative political formations. While these parties once administered the social pact between labor and capital in such a way that social welfare spending and working-class security increased, today, with capital abandoning the labor-management accord, they too are deserting what was once their chief constituency. Writing about Europe as a whole, Asbjørn Wahl says:

> The change of the character of the social-democratic parties has developed over a long time, but today's more intensified social contradictions help reveal what is hiding beneath the thin veil of political rhetoric. Where social democracy has been in power in EU countries in recent years, its leaders have been loyal executioners of brutal austerity policies, overseeing massive attacks on the welfare state and trade unions.[28]

During the massive protests in Europe in 2011, inspired by the Arab Spring and in protest against austerity when unemployment was so high in Greece, Spain, Portugal, and Italy—with youth unemployment rates near 50 percent—social democrats were remarkably silent.[29]

Because labor unions and political parties did little historically to build rank-and-file democracy and competencies or to engage members in radical, empowering education and actions, it is little wonder that the working class either abstained from voting or voted against the social democrats. "In turn this has, among other things, led to dramatically reduced support for social democrats; with few exceptions, today they are hardly represented in European governments," Wahl writes.[30] Far right, anti-immigrant, neo-fascist parties have achieved election results that would have been unimaginable even two decades ago. Fascist-like politicians, and in some cases, outright Nazis, are now mainstream in Italy, Austria, and most of the countries of the former Soviet bloc. Even in Scandinavia, social democrats have steadily lost votes, although a draconian neoliberalism hasn't taken hold there yet. In the United States, the country has sunk so far into political alienation and viciousness that someone as vile, criminal, and ignorant as Donald Trump became president.[31] For some of the same reasons, workers are forsaking labor unions, and union densities continue to fall, everywhere.

Elsewhere in the world, from Latin America to India, left-center political parties have often espoused policies that would help workers and peasants, but they have seldom delivered. Instead they have been mired in the same appeasement of capital, favored export-led development, given subsidies to foreign capital, and failed to heavily tax the wealthy or implement serious land reforms. This has been true of Brazil, Chile, Argentina, Nicaragua, and India, among many other nations. Corruption has been a common denominator in these places too. Ironically, the only government that has not gone on an austerity binge is Japan. However, militant labor unions were crushed by post–Second World War governments, aided by the United States occupation and an alliance with Japanese organized crime. Unions in Japan are typically company-controlled, and social welfare is not very generous. The high debt-financed public spending of recent decades has been due not to any social consciousness but to an effort to jump-start private spending, which has stagnated as the result of many years of economic stagnation.

―――――――――

LABOR UNIONS, LABOR POLITICAL parties, and peasant organizations have, indeed, changed the world. Yet they have not succeeded in defeating capital and moving the world on to a radically democratic and fully egalitarian trajectory. Capital is still firmly in control of production, distribution, and politics. Most of the world's income and wealth is monopolized by a small number of persons and global corporations. The advances made by the working class, broadly conceived, have proven short-lived and vulnerable to capital's power. The Soviet Union is no more, and China has moved rapidly toward a full embrace of capitalism. Social democracy is on the ropes in the Global North and has been thoroughly defeated in Great Britain and the United States. Even at its peak, social democracy did little to help workers and peasants gain control of their workplaces and land or to force a much greater equalization in the distribution of wealth. Greater income equality happened, but it is wealth that matters most.

If social democracy has never led to a full-scale assault on capitalism, what reason is there to believe that it ever could? Today, it is impossible to believe that there will be a recovery of even the modest political and economic project that labor unions and political parties once embraced and helped bring to fruition. This leaves a stark choice. Either continue to accept capitalism as a given and try to squeeze whatever crumbs capital might be willing to let fall from its table or radically change direction and begin to build a global movement that can transcend capitalism once and for all.

6—Can the Working Class Radically Change the World?

California is a state of geographical extremes: the deserts, the Sierras, the long ocean coast, and the central valleys.[1] It is a critical agricultural state, and every visitor ought to travel through the San Joaquin, Imperial, or Sacramento Valleys to see the sources of the food we eat. Go during a harvest and watch the brown-skinned men, women, and children pick the crops, the people who so many in the United States now fear and hate though without them they wouldn't have such cheap food, or any at all. Vegetables, fruits, nuts, rice, milk, meat. It is all here in great abundance, and it is produced from start to finish by the brown-skinned people. Cheap labor and subsidized capital are the basis of agriculture and most other businesses, and those that own the land aim to keep that labor cheap and those subsidies intact.

The farmworkers have waged mighty struggles to change their lives, to win better wages and some dignity. Immigrants from Japan, the Philippines, and Mexico, Chicanos, and internal migrants, those fleeing the Great Depression's Dust Bowl. Against daunting odds, they did battle with the growers, as vicious a set of employers as can be found anywhere. Here is a passage from John Steinbeck's *The Grapes of Wrath* that captures something essential if the world is to be created anew:

One man, one family driven from the land; this rusty car creaking along the highway to the west. I lost my land, a single tractor took my land. I am alone and I am bewildered. And in the night one family camps in a ditch and another family pulls in and the tents come out. The two men squat on their hams and the women and children listen. Here is the node, you who hate change and fear revolution. Keep these two squatting men apart; make them hate, fear, suspect each other. Here is the anlage of the thing you fear. Here is the zygote. For here "I lost my land is changed; a cell is split and from its splitting grows the thing you hate—"We lost our land." The danger is here, for two men are not as lonely and perplexed as one. And from this first "we" there grows a still more dangerous thing: "I have a little food" plus "I have none." If from this problem the sum is "We have a little food," the thing is on its way, the movement has direction. Only a little multiplication now, and this land, this tractor are ours. The two men squatting in a ditch, the little fire, the side-meat stewing in a single pot, the silent stone-eyed women; behind the children listening with their souls to words their minds do not understand. The night draws done. The baby has a cold. Here, take this blanket. It's wool. It was my mother's blanket—take it for the baby. This is the thing to bomb. This is the beginning—from "I" to "we."

If you who own the things people must have could understand this, you might preserve yourself. If you could separate causes from results, if you could know that Paine, Marx, Jefferson, Lenin, were results, not causes, you might survive. But that you cannot know. For the quality of owning freezes you forever into "I" and cuts you off forever from the "we."

The Western States are nervous under the beginning change. Need is the stimulus to concept, concept to action. A half-million people moving over the country; a million more restive, ready to move; ten million more feeling the first nervousness.

And tractors turning the multiple furrows in the vacant land.[2]

THE "I" AND THE "WE"

My wife and I drove north and west through parts of the San Joaquin Valley, along the irrigation ditches that help subsidize the growers. As we choked on the pesticides, we lamented that the air was so fouled we couldn't see the mountains not far to the east. The farms and ranches are enormous and highly mechanized. The research that made the machines possible is carried out at public expense in our great state universities, like the one at Davis, California—another subsidy for the growers. The labor is still cheap, too, a subsidy extorted from the government by the growers' money, which is large enough to prevent better laws and keep those on the books inadequately enforced. Also large enough to bribe and intimidate the local police, who still harass and persecute the immigrant farm laborers just as the sheriffs bullied and beat Tom Joad, the central character in Steinbeck's novel.

Our destination was a hostel in the Point Reyes National Seashore, about forty-five miles northwest of San Francisco. This is a beautiful park of steep tree-covered terrain, rolling hills and meadows, sharp bluffs overlooking the ocean, and miles of rugged coastline that includes several sand beaches. The hostel is close to Drake's Bay, named for Sir Francis Drake, who landed here in 1579. The coast that faces the Pacific Ocean directly is windswept and often damp and foggy, but Drake saw that the bay was protected from the most ferocious winds and weather, and that is why he landed there to repair his ship, the *Golden Hind*. There were native people at Point Reyes, Miwok Indians, who were gatherers and hunters, living peacefully in a land of great natural abundance. Near the Visitors' Center, volunteers have constructed a model Miwok village. At the site there is a marker on which Kathleen Smith, a contemporary Miwok, wrote in 1993:

My people have lived on the coast for at least 8,000 years. To live in physical and spiritual balance in the same small area for thousands of years without feeling the need to go somewhere else requires restraint, respect, knowledge and assurance of one's place in the world.

Once the Europeans came, the Miwok soon lost their place in the world. The Spanish missionaries forced them to abandon their traditional ways and become farm laborers. Disease and extreme culture shock killed most of them. When Mexico gained its independence, the remaining Miwok took employment where they could find it, often as servants for the rich "Californios," Mexican elite whose families had received land grants from the Spanish king. Later the United States took California from Mexico, and within a few years, the lust for gold spelled the near extinction of the Miwok (and many other groups of Indians), as the gold seekers killed them and took whatever they had left. The Miwoks' "we" was no match for the white man's "I."

After we checked into the hostel, we began to prepare our dinner in the kitchen. A young woman asked me if the water boiling in the tea kettle was mine. I said that the tea water was everyone's. She said, "Good, I didn't want to waste energy heating another kettle of water." I remarked that it was curious that people would worry about wasting a small amount of energy in a state that was a monument to waste. She looked puzzled, so I said that agriculture was a good example of waste. She said that California had the most productive agriculture in the world. This set me off on a lecture about dams, stolen water, subsidized land and water, massive use of pesticides, polluted air and water, and exploited farm workers. Measured in terms of energy in and energy out, or in terms of the costs imposed on society by California's "factories in the fields," the state's agriculture is not as productive as the Miwoks' gathering and hunting. She seemed nonplussed and went immediately into the next room to have her tea. After a few minutes, I tried to make amends for lecturing her. I asked her where she was from—Ithaca, New York, but she now lived in New York City. First year of law school at Columbia. I asked her about school and told her what a professor at the University of Pittsburgh School of Law told first-year students. He said that the first year of law school was so horrible because lawyers had to learn to be vicious by being treated viciously, just as torturers are taught to torture by being tortured. She said, well, it was good to know that every class had to go through the same treatment, including the one that would come after hers.

The woman never spoke to me again. Observing her over the next two days, we found her self-centeredness striking. She took up an inordinate amount of space in the women's dorm, strewing her clothes, including the insides of wet hiking boots, over everyone's space and in the bathroom. She tracked mud into the kitchen and was oblivious to anyone else's needs. That first evening we listened in amazement as she flirted with a German man. He was telling her about his travels around the United States. She listened, always waiting to interject something about herself. She asked him if he had traveled outside the United States and Europe. "Have you been to China?" He said no, and she replied that she had been in China, but just in Beijing, for five weeks. When he didn't ask her what she was doing in Beijing, she skillfully led the conversation toward her desired outcome. She said that she had been in China for the Olympics. The German said something that assumed she had been a spectator. She dispelled this notion by saying that this was the first time she had traveled without her medal. "Medal?" he asked. "Did you win a medal?" "Yes," she said. "Gold." Now, she had what she wanted—his unwavering admiration. The conversation degenerated from there, into a declamation of every important thing she and her family had done. She said that she loved it when at a party or a gathering of friends, someone took a picture of her holding her medal. She knew, she said, that she had "made it" when she became an entry in Wikipedia. The only blot on her brilliant persona was that somehow the law school that she wanted to attend—Stanford—had rejected her. She had to settle for Columbia. Where, no doubt, she will become firmly and permanently frozen in the "I," and cut off forever from the "we." Like so many others.

––––––––––––

CAPITALISM IS A SYSTEM of stark individualism. For the capitalist system to reproduce itself, for its outcomes to become its suppositions, people must behave in a self-interested way. Mainstream economists assume that every social actor is a maximizer of something—profits or individual satisfaction from consuming and supplying labor. They spread this view to millions of students in nearly every introductory economics class taught in universities. There is some evidence suggesting that both economics professors and students are less compassionate than others who have neither taught nor taken economics classes.[3] The primary institutions of capitalist society work in concert to inculcate the "I" in everyone, with the corollary that the "We" is detrimental to human welfare. It doesn't matter why we take self-centered actions; desire or fear serve equally well in terms of the needs of the dominant class, the imperative being the accumulation of capital.

For capitalism to end, the "I" must be suppressed and the "We" must come to the fore. This would sound strange to the gatherers and hunters who inhabited the earth for almost the entirety of human existence. They had no word for "I" and saw no difference between themselves and the natural world around them. Their lives hinged on cooperation and sharing, and their rituals and institutions helped to ensure that these were maintained. For them, the earth was a commons, the property of all. They managed their existence in ways harmonious with nature and kept the earth's metabolism in balance with their own.

Gatherers and hunters still exist but in extremely small numbers. They have been hounded out of their isolated redoubts and forced into the modern world. Some have adapted; many have died. But the reality and idea of the commons lived on, and the We was often stronger than the I. Historian Peter Linebaugh tells us,

"Scarcely a society has existed on the face of the earth which has not had at its heart the commons; the commodity with its individualism and privatization was strictly confined to the margins of the community where severe regulations punished violators."[4] Before the capitalist factory and machinery enclosed workers in walled spaces and a mechanism determined the pace of their work, before the land was made into private property, egalitarian, sharing relationships dominated much of human life. Everywhere in the world, peasants had customary rights to use common lands, for everything from gathering firewood to gleaning after harvest. Farmers periodically redivided plots of land to ensure that each family had land of roughly equal crop yields. As late as 1688, one-quarter of the total area of England and Wales was common land.[5] Even in early capitalist workplaces, skilled workers had rights to keep excess materials. In shipbuilding, the workmen had the right to keep scrap lumber. Certainly, the slaves whose labor made the great acceleration of capital accumulation in the eighteenth and nineteenth centuries possible had memories of their commons in Africa, of the "We" that dominated their lives. It was surely this that inspired their collective revolts again their "masters." The notion that the earth belonged to all was a staple of religion. "The Franciscans say *juri divino omni sunt communia*, or by divine law all things are common."[6]

What the exploitation and expropriation central to capitalism meant historically was a war, waged by law and by violence, against common ownership and customary group rights. The *I* was never natural and therefore had to be imposed. If the working class is to radically change the world, it must wage its own war against the *I* and for the *We*, learning about and building on the struggles of the past.

WHAT DOES CHANGING THE WORLD MEAN?

To transform the world, we first must have at least a general idea of the world we want to inhabit, and second, we need to know how to go about bringing such a place into existence. We can start by stating that, if capitalism is the source of the multiple woes facing the working class and its peasant comrades-in-arms, then what we desire is the antithesis of capitalist society. This would mean the end of:

- Private ownership of the means of production, including land.
- Production for profit.
- The obsession with endless economic growth.
- The exploitation of wage labor.
- The expropriation of peasant land, of urban and rural common spaces, of the labor and bodies of women, of black bodies, of all forms of patriarchy and racism.
- The private plunder of the natural world.
- Imperialism.
- The pro-capitalist role of all institutions and mechanisms that reproduce society, from family to state and from education and media to the legal system.

To put matters bluntly, the rule of capital must be terminated. Because everything that must end is central to the unceasing accumulation of capital, it is impossible to abolish any of these within the confines of this system. There can be, as we saw in chapter 4, some lessening of exploitation and expropriation, won through various forms of struggle. Wage laborers can win safer workplaces; civil rights laws can improve the lives of women and people of color; imperial wars can sometimes be averted, or poor nations can win a bit of economic independence; peasants can at least temporarily deny capital their land; a few decent politicians might win office; schools might improve some; and media might occasionally serve the public. But none of this subverts the ultimate power of the capitalist class, namely its monopoly of ownership of the world's productive property.

However, if we accept that capitalism must be superseded, it is fair to ask with what. The answer many on the left give is that we should not be in the business of designing the details of a future society. We will develop these as we attempt to change the world, seeing what works and what does not in practice. Perhaps so, but can we not at least state in general but stirring terms what we seek? At a minimum, wouldn't these demands be essential?

- A sustainable environment. What we appropriate from nature must be restored. We are headed for multiple environmental catastrophes threatening human existence. There will be no world for the working class to change if this isn't done. All economic decisions should be made with a sustainable environment a central determining factor.
- A planned economy. The anarchy of the marketplace should be replaced by conscious planning of what is produced. Periodic economic crises and unconscionable inequality are the direct results of reliance on the market. These are neither desirable nor necessary. Corporations plan, so why can't society as a whole plan?
- Socialization of as much consumption as possible, especially transportation and childcare. Living arrangements could be more collective as well. Not only will this save resources, it will socialize us in ways supportive of feelings of belonging and happiness. We are social animals not meant to live isolated lives surrounded by unnecessary privately owned consumer goods.
- Democratic worker-community control of workplaces, with, to the extent possible, the elimination of the detailed division of labor and with machinery built and introduced with social usefulness as the guiding principle. The abolition of wage labor.
- Public ownership of all the social institutions that help a society reproduce itself, from schools to media. The same should be the case for as much of the production of goods and services as possible. In many cases, cooperatives run by workers and communities should be responsible for production and distribution decisions. Local supplying is especially important for food, both in terms of transportation expenses and a healthy environment.

It will be much easier to return nutrients to the soil organically when food is grown close to where it is consumed.

- A radically egalitarian society, with equality in all spheres of life—between men and women, among all racial and ethnic groups, among all people irrespective of their gender identity or sexual preference, among and within every country with respect to work, region, and access to all social services and amenities.

- What the working class must be against is a society built upon individualism and the rule of the many by the few. No social system with inequality of power and multiple hierarchies touching most of life can be liberating, if liberation means living unalienated lives, lives in which we are not artificially and intentionally separated from one another, from what we produce, from our natures as thinking, purposive beings, and from the natural world. By contrast, the working class must be for whatever is social, collective, sharing, and unalienating.

THE MULTIPLE TERRAINS OF STRUGGLE

There are many arenas of class struggle. In each, there are both matters to fight against and to fight for. Any list must be somewhat arbitrary, but the following areas are essential.

A Statement of Principles and Commitments. Every organization and movement should have a statement of the principles and commitments that underly them. These can be general declarations, or they can take the form of demands. For example, if it is higher education that is being contested, a declaration could be "Free higher education is a right," and demands could be "Make adjunct teachers full-time professors" and "Abolish student debt." Organized black Americans might demand some form of reparations for the depredations of slavery. A specific call could be an end to the racist U.S. bail bond system.[7] Poor women might insist on the abolition of workfare and publicly-financed family allowances. "Land to the tiller," used by the Chinese revolutionaries, still resonates today in places where peasant land is being expropriated. Those organizing protests and those joining an organization can make formal commitments. In a union strike setting "I will never cross a picket line" is an obvious pledge. In anti-imperial efforts "I will not join the military" starkly proclaims that a person will not participate in the violence, including murder, that always grounds the subjugation of the people of another country by the aggressor nation. If there is a primary organization, such as a political party, the principles would take on a more general, but encompassing, character. In the United States, for example, a set of transitional demands, that is, those aimed at applying pressure to capital and could, if put into practice, pave the way for a transition to socialism, might include:

- Much shorter working hours
- Early and secure retirement
- Free universal healthcare
- An end to the notion that one must work to earn income
- An end to all corporate subsidies
- The immediate termination of all forms of discrimination
- Bans on fracking and other profit-driven environmental despoliations
- An end to the war on terror along with the closing of all U.S. military bases in other countries
- The abolition of the present prison system
- Free schooling at all levels
- Open borders combined with the termination of U.S. financial support for oppressive governments
- Community-based policing
- Transfer of abandoned buildings and land to communities and groups that will put them to socially useful purposes[8]

Every proclamation of principles must contain strong commitments to ending patriarchy and racism. These exist as such important cleavages within the working class that they can never be ignored.

Statements and commitments are rare today, but that makes them all the more important. People naturally gravitate toward organizations and leaders who have standards from which they do not deviate. Former U.S. president Barack Obama said that when he was a candidate he would put on walking shoes and join striking picketers. But he never did. He often said one thing and then did the opposite. Mao Zedong, on the other hand, said that land would go to the peasants who worked it, and that is what was done. Whom do you think has, to this day, more committed admirers? Karl Marx stuck to his fundamental principles no matter the consequences. His analyses changed as he learned more about how societies functioned. But he never changed his mind about the nature of capitalism, and he devoted his life to destroying capital's power. No wonder he is held in the highest esteem by tens of millions of people.

Radical Education. In discussing "commoning"—the act of doing things in common, such as working in a community garden or caring for a forest that is used by an indigenous group of peasants in India—Peter Linebaugh says, "Communal values must be taught, and renewed, continuously."[9] Parents, churches, civic organizations, and the like might try to inculcate such values in the children and members, and when people engage in collective struggles, they learn them. However, it takes more than these things to make collective ways of thinking an integral part of our lives, providing, in effect, a compass that gives us direction. Radical, critical, and continued education is needed. It will not only help to put our lives and actions into context, but it also will give us a better understanding of what needs to be done in the future. Through it, we can learn to analyze our individual histories, to, in effect, examine and pass judgments on ourselves.

There are many elements in radical education. First, there must be a relationship of mutual respect between teacher and student. That is, both must feel part of a larger project, the liberation of humanity from the shackles of capitalism. While the teachers have specialized knowledge, they learn from their students in a give-and-take process of democratic discussion. If education isn't egalitarian, how can we expect anything else to be? Second, those who teach must, whatever the topic, direct the conversation toward the nature of the system. A science teacher can ask, what influences the questions science poses? How is science funded? Is what a scientist does value-free? Then, pose a question such as, why is so little government funding given to researchers who want to know the possible consequences of genetically modified organisms? In social sciences, one could ask how likely it would be for a scholar to earn a PhD if the thesis subject is "How can a guerilla army best defeat the U.S. armed forces in Iraq?"

In labor education, the question "What is capitalism?" is paramount. The teacher must try to show that this is a system that rests on a bedrock of exploitation and expropriation. Even if a class is about a practical matter, such as labor law or organizing a union, the nature of society is critical to explaining what the law is, why unions are necessary, and so forth. In all organizations, whether they are fighting for a cleaner environment, better housing, lower rents, converting abandoned urban land to community gardens, ending theft of peasant lands, socialized healthcare, ending racism and patriarchy, or the termination of wars and imperialism, capitalism must be central to the teaching and learning. It might seem that teaching the nature of capitalism is a daunting task, but peasants have been taught the rudiments of the three volumes of Karl Marx's magnum opus, *Capital*. Nothing is impossible.

Third, every entity seeking radical change must have an education component integral to its operation. Labor unions and peasant organizations need to set aside time and resources for this. Most unions in the United States have little or no member education, much less radical education. This is one reason why the rank and file are alienated from the leadership. Not a few union officers fear an educated membership, which might decide to replace them. Political parties and formations, Occupy Wall Street–types of movements, antiwar organizations, anti-racist and anti-patriarchy movements need education efforts as well, ones that become permanently built into their structures. Planning actions, carrying them out, assessing successes and failures—all are vital subjects of education for members and participants.

Fourth, radical education is about making connections. One organization's projects are connected to those of every other group; each person's life is part of a larger whole. For example, some employers, especially in restaurants, have a work requirement known as "clopening," in which the same workers who close late at night have to get to work early the next morning to open the place for business. Suppose a movement developed to end this practice. The damage done to workers by clopening—lack of sleep and the attendant mental and physical stresses—could be directly tied to the need for shorter hours and more free time, such as vacations and personal days. This, in turn, could lead to the question of what gives an employer the power to make clopening mandatory and, more generally, to decide how we labor and with what intensity. Or imagine that an urban coalition of fair housing groups is trying to force a city to stop giving tax subsidies to the builders of luxury apartments. This specific struggle could be connected to the need for high-quality public housing, as well as to the societal benefits of stopping the gentrification of working-class neighborhoods.[10]

Racism, patriarchy, and imperialism are all connected to exploitation and expropriations, as is climate change. Radical education, by showing why this is so, can help to ignite the class consciousness necessary to change the world.

Fifth, whatever the setting, begin with the lives, the daily experiences, of the students. Education scholar and teacher Ira Shor

> begins a writing class with community college students by examining the chairs on which they are sitting. He first has them carefully describe the chairs, forcing them to look at them carefully and slowly. However, the description is just the beginning; through discussion and more writing, Shor and his students

discover the chair's origin within the economy and the cultural assumptions behind its production (e.g., why it's so uncomfortable!). Ultimately, the students, mostly through their own efforts, are able to divest the chair of its commodity fetishism by totally understanding it in relation to the society which produced it. The complete exercise not only demystifies the chair itself, but gives a striking experimental demonstration of how to analyze capitalism and of the dialectical method of understanding one's own environment.[11]

Labor educator and *Monthly Review* co-founder Leo Huberman gives a striking example of radical and critical teaching. He asks his worker-students a series of simple questions about their lives as working men and women.

Where do you work? Why do you work? Does the man who owns the factory work alongside you? Have you ever seen the stockholders of the corporation working in the plant? But you all agreed you had to work in order to live; now you tell me there are some people who live without working. How come? Then there are two groups of people in our society. One group, to which you belong, lives by . . . ? And the other group to which your employer belongs lives by . . . ?

The questions continue until the teacher and the students see that profits are unearned and come at the expense of the sweat and tears of those who perform their labor. It's a brilliant exercise, eliciting from the students the most basic element of the work lives and generating a lively discussion of what they might do about it.[12]

Sixth, radical educators should teach in such a way that some of the students will themselves take what they have learned and teach it to others. The goal is to create organic intellectuals, that is, people from the working class who become capable of spreading the word the way Leo Huberman did. Some of the prisoners I once taught took my lecture diagrams, which I had copied and distributed, back to their cell blocks where they used them to teach fellow inmates. Similarly, union members can teach their brothers and sisters. Not only does this greatly increase the number of teachers, but it also breaks down the hierarchy between instructors and pupils.

Agriculture, Peasants, Farmworkers, and the Environment. A radically changed world cannot come to exist if the environment is wrecked beyond repair and if there is not enough food to eat. Capitalist agriculture is large-scale, machine- and chemical-intensive, overloaded with pesticides, and destructive of the quality of air, water, and land. Billions of pounds of pesticides are used every year worldwide, most of which end up in the air, soil, and water.[13] Our industrial agriculture is based upon extensive use of fossil fuels, and a great deal of land is used to produce crops not for human consumption but for animal feed and biofuels. Agriculture contributes considerably to global warming. Ecology writer Ian Angus informs us that "In 2007, the U.S. food system, from farm to table, used 16 percent of all of the country's energy."[14] This energy derives from fossil fuels, the main contributor to global warming. In terms of energy expended in production and energy generated by the crops, it is incredibly inefficient, even compared to food production in gathering and hunting societies. "It now takes more energy to produce food than we obtain from eating it: every calorie of food energy requires 10 calories of fossil energy.."[15] Most of the vegetables, fruits, meats, and fish that are agriculture's end products are heavily processed before being consumed, which means that they are stripped of nutrients and adulterated with thousands of additives, from coloring to sweeteners.

Modern agriculture gives the world an enormous amount of food, but its distribution is as unequal as are income and wealth. The well-off have high daily caloric intakes, while the poor are food-deprived. Estimates of the number of hungry in the world vary, ranging from about 850 million to more than two billion people.[16] At the same time, peasants and small farmers often live on the edge of calamity or are unable to eke out a living. They are being driven from their farms by land-grabbing capitalists, aided by both governments and international financial organizations like the World Bank and International Monetary Fund. Land has become a valuable commodity, and speculators, including hedge fund managers, have been on a buying spree in the Global South, often letting their property lie idle while they wait for the price to rise. The sale of the land has frequently been preceded by violence and death.[17] The 866 million farmworkers, many of them former or current peasants, suffer short life expectancies, pesticide poisoning, and state-sponsored violence whenever they attempt to organize. Their working conditions are extraordinarily harsh, and their prospects for decent lives nonexistent.

Agriculture is organized now on a factory model, with enormous operational scale, the use of subcontractors, maximum production control and uniformity, with little concern for either the quality of the food or the health of workers and the earth. Animals such as cattle, hogs, and chickens are raised in grotesquely inhumane conditions, overfed with food laced with growth supplements so that they reach maturity as quickly as possible. They are sent to market in an unhealthy state more often than consumers imagine.[18]

A radical change of the world requires that agriculture be revolutionized, away from giant "factories in the fields" that poison and overheat the environment, leave so many hungry, and maximally exploit and expropriate the working class. This is a primary necessity, because if the earth is ruined and humanity cannot be adequately fed, then there is no hope at all. Fortunately, we do know how to organize a food system that avoids what is happening now.

Peasants, small farmers, and farmworkers have the skills and experience to produce food in an earth-sustaining, productive, and collective manner. They are already doing this and organizing against industrial agriculture and for smaller-scale, more local, and ecologically nourishing food production and distribution. It is essential that the working class support such endeavors and engage in them wherever possible. Worker-peasant alliances will be needed in the Global South, and even in the Global North. Following are some examples.

Most wage workers live in or near cities, the consequence of the "metabolic rift" that Marx and others have analyzed. This results from the advent of capitalist agriculture in the countryside and the rigid separation of rural and urban areas, with the latter dedicated to the consumption of what is created in the former. One way to heal this rift is for food to be produced in urban areas, on abandoned land, in community gardens, on rooftops, on balconies and porches, and in vertical farms.

Cuba provides the best example of this approach.[19] After the 1990–91 demise of the Soviet Union, which had provided Cuba with its oil, the country embarked upon an ambitious plan of farming without fossil fuels and mechanization. Research had been done and some experience gained before this, but now the nation embraced organic, non-mechanized farming wholeheartedly. Special attention was given to urban areas, most notably Havana, where various types of small-scale organic agriculture were employed. The result is a network of plots and farms inside the city, producing fresh vegetables and fruits, supplying seeds, creating thousands of jobs, generating income, and providing markets for agricultural inputs made elsewhere in the country. Some units are privately owned; others are organized as cooperatives. Food is consumed directly by the producers, sold in markets (selling to tourists provides foreign exchange for imports), or sold at state-mandated low prices to schools, hospitals, and other social entities. Education, training, and management is both centralized and decentralized, the motto being, "Produce while learning, teach while producing, and learn while teaching." Cuba has a well-educated, learn-by-doing population that is used to engaging in collective efforts. There are many persons knowledgeable about agroecological science and methods, with experts willing to learn from those who have long practiced traditional farming. The expectation is that production will be aimed at satisfying needs and not the capital accumulation imperative of capitalist economies.

Hardships imposed by the harsh sanctions placed upon the island by the United States have hardened Cubans against adversity.[20] It is remarkable that they have managed to build an urban agriculture that now can satisfy the fresh fruits and vegetable needs of Havana, a city with two million inhabitants. It is not miraculous, but it shows that capitalist industrial agriculture is not a human imperative. There are alternatives.

Urban agriculture is not unique to Cuba. It is done in many cities, including some in the United States. In Detroit, abandoned land has been converted to food production, organized collectively by community activists:

> The Oakland Avenue Farmers' Market in Detroit's North End is one of those small-but-mighty neighborhood markets that accomplishes a lot with a little. Each Saturday, it offers fresh fruit, vegetables, and other healthy foods in a historically low-income and black neighborhood where such options aren't readily available. Just as important is its contribution to the neighborhood's economy. Most of the profits generated since it launched in 2009 fund the adjacent Oakland Avenue Farm. That operation provides 13 full- and part-time jobs that pay a living wage—also rare in the North End—in addition to teaching residents to grow and cook their own food. So supporting the Oakland Market is a small contribution to the neighborhood's economy.[21]

As in Cuba, women have been at the forefront of urban farming in Detroit, as have people of color. There are more than 1,000 community gardens in the city, part of a movement spearheaded by the late radical philosopher and activist, Grace Lee Boggs, who

> sees urban gardening as the beginning of a major shift in the way we feed ourselves as well as a way to connect generations in a widely inclusive movement. . . .
>
> "There's a group on the east side called Feed 'Em Freedom

Growers; if you don't have food you can't be free. Detroit has over 1,000 community gardens. Urban agriculture started very simply with some African-American women seeing some vacant lots. That's how big changes take place, with small changes. Important changes always start from the bottom up. We think they come from the top, or start with millions of people. No, they start when some people respond to the historical context and do what needs to be done. That's how revolution takes place."[22]

Vertical farms are another way to produce food in cities:

No. 212 Rome Street, in Newark, New Jersey, used to be the address of Grammer, Dempsey & Hudson, a steel-supply company. It was like a lumberyard for steel, which it bought in bulk from distant mills and distributed in smaller amounts, mostly to customers within a hundred-mile radius of Newark. It sold off its assets in 2008 and later shut down. In 2015, a new indoor-agriculture company called AeroFarms leased the property. It had the rusting corrugated-steel exterior torn down and a new building erected on the old frame. Then it filled nearly seventy thousand square feet of floor space with what is called a vertical farm. The building's ceiling allowed for grow tables to be stacked twelve layers tall, to a height of thirty-six feet, in rows eighty feet long. The vertical farm grows kale, bok choi, watercress, arugula, red-leaf lettuce, mizuna, and other baby salad greens.[23]

The technology of vertical farming is relatively simple, but the care of the plants is complicated and requires sophisticated knowledge of biology and electronic communication. However, these things can be mastered; a small-scale version of a vertical farm has been installed in an elementary school in Newark, where staff and students keep it up and running.[24]

The advantages of urban farming are many. It provides food for local consumption and generates some employment. From it can come backward and forward linkages. Farms need inputs (backward linkages), some of which might be supplied locally. They can also be connected to farmers' markets, grocery stores, schools, hospitals, and prisons (forward linkages). The markets, schools, and stores could be run by worker cooperatives. Through such activity, the working class learns forms of collective self-help, gaining confidence in its capacity to organize production. What is more, the "We" is central, and is reinforced continually. Moreover, urban agriculture gets workers closer to nature, and with a better grasp of nature's metabolism they are more likely to heed the warnings of ecological doom.

In both the Global North and the Global South, numerous small farmers and peasants have embraced agroecological farming, using practices thousands of years old as well as modern science-based techniques. There are many and varied ways to farm agroecologically, but the goal is to create balance between humans and nature, constantly replenishing the earth with the nutrients necessary for continuous production of food. Some of the ways to do this include abandoning chemical fertilizers by using legumes to fix nitrogen in the soil; use of natural pest controls; limited tilling of the soil; planting a variety of mutually supporting fruits and vegetables and avoiding monocropping; mixing crop farming and animal husbandry, with manure from the animals used for the plants; drip irrigation in dry climates; water-capturing techniques; mosaic landscapes in which farm and non-farm habitats such as forests, streams, and wetlands are interspersed to increase biodiversity; control of water runoff and erosion through, among other things, planting of cover crops; and many others. Such farming shows considerable productivity gains.[25] When combined with cooperation and collective production, social consciousness can change sharply.

LIKE EVERY RADICAL CHANGE, altering the way food is produced and distributed meets with resistance from capital. Class struggle around agriculture is widespread. In the Amazon River basin, peasants have been fighting against the construction of massive dams, which destroy traditional common areas and farm fields, with accompanying environmental damage both downstream and upstream from the dams.[26] Maoist political parties and their military wings have organized Indian forest dwellers to contest land grabs. At various times over the past fifty years, guerillas have secured control over indigenous territories and helped to build cooperative agriculture, following the process begun by Mao's Red Army in China.[27]

In Brazil, a Landless Workers Movement (MST are its Portuguese initials) has been in operation since the early 1980s. Now, with more than one million members, it has orchestrated the seizure of unoccupied and unproductive lands throughout the country. Peasants are settled—several hundred thousand to date—on these parcels, food is grown, and a network of schools, cooperatives, and credit unions are put in place. "The movement has ratified over 2,000 settlements, settling over 370,000 families with an estimated 80,000 more awaiting settlement, established a network of approximately 2,000 primary and secondary schools, partnered with 13 public universities, 160 rural cooperatives, 4 credit unions, and started food processing plants, and retail outlets."[28] The MST's slogan is "Occupy, Resist, Produce," a wonderful summary of the need to combine protest with collective self-help that satisfies people's material needs.[29]

In the U.S. state of Florida, in the farmworker town of Immokalee, the Coalition of Immokalee Workers (CIW), a community-based labor group, has forced some of the nation's largest tomato-buying fast food chains to pay a premium for tomatoes picked by its members. This money then goes to the workers. Aided by a national network of "churches, students, and consumer activists," the CIW organized boycotts of the restaurants, which helped win concessions from the chains, who then sign on to the CIW's Fair Food Program. This contains provision of "worker-to-worker education sessions, a worker-triggered complaint resolution mechanism, and the establishment of health and safety committees on every participating farm." The group also investigates, publicizes, and aids in the prosecution of slavery rings that supply workers to unscrupulous growers.[30]

Workers and peasants everywhere have an obligation to support these struggles and all like them, with publicity, mutual assistance, and funds when possible. Whatever improvements peasants, farmers, and farmworkers make in their lives, the healthier is the earth. And the more livable rural areas are, the more they will attract new residents, including the return of peasants from the degrading urban slums that are now their homes. As this happens, the metabolic rift that separated people from the land in the first place can begin to heal.

Labor Unions. Labor unions have been a principal response by workers to capital's exploitation. They are necessary defense agents, and as long as capitalism exists, they will form. In chapter 4, we saw the extent to which they have managed to change the world, and in chapter 5, we critiqued their shortcomings. What might they do to attack the power of the class enemy more directly?

If unions mirror corporations in their structures, which all too many do, there isn't much hope that they will confront capital. And this is all the more the case if they have entered into a compact with employers that views the two sides as cooperators interested primarily in the profitability of the owners' businesses. This strategy has failed, the proof being in the deteriorating working conditions and life circumstances of union members and the sharp drop in union densities during the period in which partnership has marked much of the labor movement worldwide. To begin to reverse course, then, labor unions must become democratic, run by the membership, and they must abandon labor-management cooperation schemes. Since it is unlikely that current leaders will seek to do either of these things, the only way forward is to get rid of the leadership. In the United States, a perusal of the magazine *Labor Notes* shows that there have been frequent attempts by rank-and-file activists to take control of their unions and put them on a democratic and militant path. A few have been successful, most have not. No doubt the fear of such insurgencies has made some unions willing to mobilize members and take on the companies with strikes, picketing, and boycotts. But reform has proved a daunting task, similar to efforts by political advocates to move the Democratic Party to the left. Those in power seldom want to relinquish control, and they will be as ruthless as necessary to beat back rivals.[31] Still, labor rebellions have been successful, at all levels of unions. Corrupt criminal leadership was defeated in both the Teamsters and the United Mine Workers, for example, and though the rank-and-file victors were subsequently defeated or weakened, neither union is as awful as it once was.[32] In addition, sometimes revolt has taken the form of a new union, one that breaks away from the parent organization. Or, if a group of workers have no representation and no existing union is willing to help them organize, they might establish an independent union. Again in the United States, an example of the former is the National Union of Healthcare Workers (NUHW). Tired of the Service Employees International Union's (SEIU) top-down management, its embrace of labor-management cooperation and sweetheart deals with employers, its frequent impositions of trusteeships (the national union takes over the running of a local union) on recalcitrant locals with rebellious and independent leaders, and outright corruption, the NUHW broke away from SEIU in 2009.

Before asking what a democratic union looks like and what it should do, it is proper to say that there are now unions that work in a democratic manner. In the United States, the best example is the United Electrical Workers, an independent labor union that has the distinction of being kicked out of both the AFL and the CIO. Its national office and locals rest on the will of the members. It does not make deals with employers, and it has never been tainted with corruption. Officer salaries and expenses are strictly controlled, and its constitution is a model of democratic principles that the union has adhered to through good times and bad.[33] Other U.S. unions have served their members well, too. The same is true in Europe and many other countries. The overall trajectory, how-ever, has been toward bureaucratic, undemocratic structures and an increasingly unwarranted faith in labor-capital compromise.[34]

Democracy means more than voting. The structure of the union must be democratic. There should be direct ballot casting by all the members for any office, as opposed to convention delegates, usu-ally chosen by the leadership, voting for those same leaders, as is common in many U.S. unions. Term limits for officers are essential. No advantage of any kind should be proffered to incumbents seek-ing reelection. Strict limits should be placed on the salaries of union officers, and a careful open audit of expenses should be routine. The rank and file should participate in all union activities, from planning for negotiations, setting demands, strike preparation, and the strik-ing and picketing. Union meetings should be open to all members, especially those with home responsibilities (almost always women), and also held at convenient times. Meeting discussions should be open, and criticisms should be welcomed and debated. Special atten tion should be paid, in all aspects of the union, to the concerns and needs of racial and ethnic minorities, as well as LGBT members. Retirees should be encouraged to take part in all union actions.

If a rank-and-file uprising is successful, a breakaway union is founded, or an independent union is created, and even if these result in more democracy, it is still necessary to ask: Democracy for what? What are the principles and goals of the organization? The NUHW lists these as its core beliefs:

- A strong union is led by its members.
- Worker power is the foundation of a just society.
- Quality patient care requires that caregivers have a voice in their workplaces and are protected from retaliation.
- Healthcare is a human right.[35]

This is a good preliminary set of principles. But more needs to be said and done. First, education must be a priority. Compulsory classes should greet new members, teaching them about the union's history and that of the labor movement as a whole. And regular short courses, summer schools, and longer learning experiences should be made available, with at least some courses required to maintain membership. In these classes, the construction of a broader array of principles and aspirations can be developed. Several come to mind:

- An examination of racism and patriarchy. The objectives here are ending discrimination in the union, building greater solidarity, compelling the employer to behave in a nondiscriminatory manner, and leading the union to play a positive role in combating these divisions in the community and society.
- A study of imperialism and militarism. For unions in the Global North, the purpose of this would be to build an understanding of the role of their governments and employers in subjugating the peoples of the Global South, and of the past complicity of unions in this. A radical labor movement cannot become a reality unless it is adamantly opposed to imperial wars, arms production and sales, the infiltration of the military into local economies and daily life, the patriotism of flags and national anthems, the mantra that we must all support the troops. In the Global North, nationalism is a disease that impedes the global working-class solidarity essential for human liberation. Unfortunately, it is so deeply embedded in the institutional structure of capitalist society that the task of eliminating it is formidable. Yet, if the effort isn't made, there is no hope of the working class changing the world. In the Global South, the angle of vision on these subjects will be different, although the ruling classes here often act in lockstep with those in the Global North.
- A serious discussion of the multiple environmental crises we face. If these aren't working-class issues, what are? In both Egypt and Syria, extreme drought, following years of austerity economic policies, growing inequality, and public corruption triggered revolts by workers and peasants during the Arab Spring that began in December 2010.[36]

The last point merits further discussion. The weather events in Egypt and Syria are surely harbingers of things to come. Furthermore, global warming is a workplace issue. Ecology professor and writer Andreas Malm writes:

> Physical labour makes the body warm. If it takes place under the sun or inside facilities without advanced air-conditioning systems, excessively high temperatures will make the sweat flow more profusely and the bodily powers sag, until the worker suffers heat exhaustion or worse. This will not be an ordeal for the average software developer or financial adviser. But for people who pick vegetables, build skyscrapers, pave roads, drive buses, sew clothes in poorly ventilated factories or mend cars in slum workshops, it already is; and the bulk of exceptionally hot working days are now anthropogenic in nature. With every little rise in average temperatures on Earth, thermal conditions in millions of workplaces around the world shift further, primarily in the tropical and subtropical regions where the majority of the working population—some four billion people—live their days. For every degree, a greater chunk of output will be lost, estimated to reach more than a third of total production after four degrees: in this heat, workers simply cannot keep up the same pace.[37]

Given the magnitude of impending disasters, labor must make the environment a major concern. This means opposing all corporate and public actions that exacerbate global warming, the poisoning of air, soil, and water, and the extinction of species, among others. When construction unions lobby for ruinous shale oil pipelines, as happened in the United States, other unions must speak out and condemn such self-serving deeds.

As democratic unions strengthen and their principles and goals become more class-conscious, they will naturally ally themselves with like-minded unions and community groups. In this way, a labor movement worthy of the name can begin and grow, one concerned with the entirety of the working class, including those in the reserve army of labor and the informal sector.

A union's most important immediate concern is with its members' welfare. Here the question of "democracy for what?" can take concrete form. Labor-management cooperation should be immediately and permanently rejected, replaced by an adversarial relationship that makes no concessions to management. Instead the union makes demands that challenge capital's control of the workplace. Higher wages are always on the table, but so must be shorter hours, more paid time off, full parental leave for both parents (for at least a few months), a safe and nontoxic work environment, active union participation in decisions related to both technology and work intensity, an unrestricted right to strike over any issue, a shortened grievance resolution procedure (with rank-and-file participation at all levels), the right not to cross picket lines while on employer-related business, and high monetary penalties for plant closures and relocations. Whatever makes laboring less alienated and weakens capital's control should be vigorously and relentlessly pursued. Unions should never allow the employer to play one plant off against another, much less cooperate in this, as the United Auto Workers has done.[38] Strong protections for women and racial and ethnic minorities should be part of every contract. When a union faces a multi-plant employer, or more than one employer, it should organize coordinated communications and tactics among the officers on the shop floor, office, or store. Solidarity must be more than a word, and an injury to any worker should anger every sister and brother.

———

WHILE DEMOCRACY, PRINCIPLES, and radical goals are necessary everywhere, unions in the Global South encounter some special choices and difficulties. There, wage laborers need to consider the needs and actions of peasants. In Brazil, for example, unions felt they should lead the way in land reform issues, rather than the Landless Workers Movement. However, "Many in large Brazilian labor unions believed the fight for agrarian reform should take place within union ranks—but unions didn't accept landless farmers as members."[39] Even if one were to argue that this was shortsighted, it still didn't preclude active union support for what the farmers and peasants were doing. In India, labor unions have failed to offer full-throated support for the Maoist rebellions in the countryside.[40] A worker-peasant alliance is essential for the working class to change the world, and until wage laborers embrace it, such change will not happen.

In many countries, attempts to unionize put workers at risk of arrest, imprisonment, or death. In Colombia, murders of labor activists have been routine. "Anti-union violence has been endemic to Colombia for decades, with roughly 3,000 organizers killed by assassins and paramilitaries over the last quarter-century [roughly 1989 to 2014]. . . . In fact, more than half of all murders for union-organizing activity worldwide take place here. But as murder numbers have dropped in recent years, the nature of the violence is changing, and there's evidence to suggest that the Colombian state is complicit in the repression."[41] In China, the state allows only official unions, and these are not independent agents of the working class. Attempts to confront global corporations like Walmart with their own unions put employees in the government's crosshairs. Arrests and jail sentences are common. In such onerous conditions, labor must often operate in secret, underground, and try to take actions in such large numbers that the state finds it hard to suppress. Strict media censorship further hampers the working class. Despite these barriers, workers still rebel, often with mass demonstrations and militancy. Sometimes, they win demands made on the companies and even secure concessions from the government.

IT IS IMPORTANT TO UNDERSTAND that, despite the problems of unions and labor movements, workers have continued to organize and act. Today, around the world, in France, Greece,

Spain, Portugal, Italy, China, India, Algeria, Indonesia, South Africa, nearly everywhere in the world, there have been strikes, demonstrations, land, building, and factory occupations, sabotage, and open warfare. Even in the United States, as journalist Michelle Chen reports, there has been an upsurge of interest in unionization among younger workers, who face downward economic mobility and challenging life prospects. What is most encouraging is the unity these new unionists are showing across gender, racial, and ethnic lines.[42] These efforts show signs of intensifying as capitalism suffers recurring crises and shows itself as unable to satisfy the most basic needs of billions of human beings. There is certainly a base for the construction of a new world.

THERE ARE UNION-LIKE GROUPS that also take up the cause of the working class. The Coalition of Immokalee Workers, discussed above, is an example. The CIW is a "worker center," of which there are many in the United States. Workers' centers are community-based organizations, some independent and some affiliated with the official labor movement. Many organize around immigrant issues, while others function as de facto unions. The Chinese Staff & Workers' Association in New York City combats wage theft and other violations of labor laws in restaurants and garment sweatshops. It provides education and related materials for members and has won a great deal of backpay for aggrieved workers. It builds solidarity by demanding that anyone it helps aids others in turn. Labor activist Elly Leary, in an essay about the CIW, argues:

> Non-union working-class organizations dealing with worker issues have a central place in the labor movement. Generally smaller in size than many union locals, workers' centers have the flexibility to experiment with different methods of engaging workers and training leaders. Furthermore, given the right's success in creating an anti-union climate (by popularizing the view

that unions are obsolete), centers can appeal to broad sections of the working class that unions may have a difficult time reaching. Anti-union laws and recent decisions by courts and the National Labor Relations Board have narrowed how unions can fight and what they can win. If we add to this the frustrating discussion currently going on in the trade union movement about its future, workers' centers seem to hold great promise. But we shouldn't throw out the baby with the bathwater. If our movement were to rely exclusively on workers' centers to organize the working class for fundamental social change, we would find that there aren't enough centuries to build at this pace. Nonetheless, workers' centers are an essential basis for struggle.[43]

Cooperation between unions and worker centers could be a strategy to rebuild labor movements. Suppose that in every large and medium-size town, a worker center was opened for restaurant labor. Any cook, dishwasher, or server could join from any place that prepared food. The center would be a space in which workers could meet one another and discuss common problems, at work and at home. The center could provide education, useful materials, advice for dealing with employers, and so forth. It could spearhead organizing drives at particular establishments or, if there were enough members, sponsor employer-wide unionization. Language study could be provided for those, of whom there might be many, who are not literate in the country's language. Similar centers could be built for other occupations and establishments. Mutual support could be a prerequisite for joining a center. Regional and national coordinating bodies might naturally follow from the successes of local centers.

Labor and Politics. What has been said about unions can be applied with equal force to labor's political path, so just a few points can be made here. First, substantive equality must prevail in political entities, just as it must in labor unions. This means that social democratic parties will have to be replaced by democratic working-class parties. Here too, democracy is more than voting. Those in the party must run it. It must have radical principles and have radical goals. It must be built from the ground up, with those at the top responsible to those at the bottom. Perhaps the course followed in Venezuela (discussed below) is a good model. Local assemblies seize the political initiative and then the assemblies begin to consolidate in larger geographical areas, culminating in a national party. These could then ally themselves with similar parties in other countries. At each level, the forming groups would commit to a set of principles. Second, working-class political parties can contend for state power, but in most cases this isn't likely to result in electoral victory. Education could then be the modus operandi of the party. In any case, radical pressure on the existing state should be exerted at all times. If special circumstances allow electoral victory, radical goals should be enunciated and movement toward achieving them should begin immediately. The collective power of the working class should be the weapon employed to do this—mass demonstrations and strikes, for example. The military must be challenged and most of its officers must be demobilized. There could be cases in which a party has a military wing, in parts of the Global South, for example, and then revolutionary warfare can be considered, as in Nepal in the early part of this century or in the Indian countryside, which has been happening over the past several decades.

Another model for working-class politics is the Richmond Progressive Alliance (RPA), a labor-community coalition in the U.S. city of Richmond, California. The RPA functions year-round as a political entity, with a dues-paying, diverse base and a multi-issue agenda, but it actively runs candidates for local office. Since 2004, its nominees have won many offices, including mayor. It operates on a democratic basis, and it has regularly debated and found ways to maintain and increase both the diversity of its membership and the breadth and depth of its program. It works with community groups and local labor unions to address issues of great concern to the working class. The RPA and the local government, over which its victorious candidates have considerable influence, have fought for rent control, pollution abatement at the large Chevron oil refinery, against police brutality and for a community-based model of policing, against the harassment of immigrants by ICE (Immigration and Customs Enforcement), and many other issues. The RPA has also taken stances on national and international matters, such as demanding an end to the blockade of Cuba by the U.S, government.

The RPA does not take corporate money nor do its office seekers. It is also independent of the Democratic Party. One of its leaders, longtime union activist Mike Parker, suggests that the Richmond model could be applied to many towns and cities, and he notes that while local politics cannot solve many critical problems, what people learn fighting for the betterment of the places in which they live usually translates into concern for such matters and a greater willingness to speak out and organize around them. Consciousness, in other words, stems from action, and study and education informs what people are willing to do.[44] Were RPA organizations to form in many places, they could coalesce into regional and national political bodies.

Third, there is no reason for a working-class political project to exist unless its aim is the defeat of capital. Demands should be radical and principled, and they should be adhered to. Tactical compromise might sometimes be necessary, but this can never be a strategy. We know that coping with a rapidly warming planet and many other environmental catastrophes will be central to all politics. A labor party, therefore, must address ecological questions directly and forcefully. Andreas Malm offers ten policies that could be implemented to begin the mitigation of ongoing ecological destruction:

1. Enforce a complete moratorium on all new facilities for extracting coal, oil, or natural gas.
2. Close down all power plants running on such fuels.
3. Draw 100 percent of electricity from non-fossil sources, primarily wind and solar.

4. Terminate the expansion of air, sea, and road travel; convert road and sea travel to electricity and wind; ration remaining air travel to ensure a fair distribution until it can be completely replaced with other means of transport.
5. Expand mass transit systems on all scales, from subways to intercontinental high-speed trains.
6. Limit the shipping and flying of food and systematically promote local supplies.
7. End the burning of tropical forests and initiate massive programs for reforestation.
8. Refurbish old buildings with insulation and require all new ones to generate their own zero-carbon power.
9. Dismantle the meat industry and move human protein requirements toward vegetable sources.
10. Pour public investment into the development and diffusion of the most efficient and sustainable renewable energy technologies, as well as technologies for carbon dioxide removal.[45]

No doubt these policies will seem utopian to many people. But they are necessary, Malm points out, just to get us started on the road to a sustainable environment. Surely a radical working-class party, especially in the Global North, which is responsible for most of the devastation, should be expected to make such demands central to its work.

Fourth, labor parties can support and partly fund the mutual aid efforts workers and peasants initiate. Some of these are described below in the subsection, Direct Action. Worker education schools, cooperatives, community gardens, and day-care centers, for example, should be supported by these parties, and attacks on them should be countered politically.

Racism and Patriarchy. These terrains of class struggle must be attacked in every organization and in each attempt by workers and peasants to challenge capital and build alternatives to it. What fights racism and patriarchy challenges the central features of the system: exploitation and expropriation. How can workers be organized if there are racial and gender tensions among those seeking representation by a union? How can a guerilla war be won unless women are full participants? How can a workplace be egalitarian if homes are not? What good is a left-wing party if its leaders assault women with impunity?

It is an unworthy argument that says race and gender are mere identities, whereas class is a social relationship. Writer and political analyst Richard Seymour puts it well when he says:

> To me, it's straightforward. Class is a social relationship that is structured by race, gender, sexuality, nationality, and a whole range of other determinations. Race is the modality in which millions of people inhabit their class experience. Their "identity politics" will often be the precise way in which they fight a class struggle. Black Lives Matter, a struggle against the racialized violence of the capitalist state, is an example of that, and it is of benefit to the whole working class if it succeeds. Now, what would be implied if we socialists were to write off such a movement, which has already had such an impact culturally? Surely it would be that at best we are purists who are incapable of intelligent political intervention in real-life situations, at worst that we subscribe to some spurious "color-blind" politics.
>
> What is more, "identity" is never as straightforward as a label. It is a process, "identification." To identify myself is to identify myself with others, to say who I am like, who I have interests in common with. Some identifications are potentially more expansive, more universal, than others. The identity of a black woman prisoner is more conducive to solidarity and radical change than that of a white Republican congressman.[46]

It is also wrong to claim that though race and gender are important, class is more so, and everything else must wait upon its resolution. This is a certain way never to face racism and patriarchy directly. It is true, for example, that if a U.S. union wins a fixed-dollar wage increase for all the members of one of its bargaining units, black workers and women will gain the most in percentage terms because they have been the lowest paid. But what does this do to change the culture within the union, one that has had a history of racism and patriarchy? This will do nothing to make the union's leadership less white and male or make white workers less racist and men less sexist in their behavior. Black workers had to take the Steelworkers' union to court to end the structural racism embedded in its negotiated seniority system.[47] Nor will wage gains prevent a union from being less attentive to the grievances of black and women workers. The same arguments apply to LGBT workers. During the late 1960s, black automobile workers in Detroit formed an organization called the Dodge Revolutionary Union Movement (DRUM), which later expanded into a more encompassing movement, the League of Revolutionary Black Workers. Black workers conducted wildcat strikes, but they also targeted their union, the United Auto Workers (UAW), which had a stellar reputation as a supporter of the civil rights movement and was considered one of the most progressive labor unions in the nation. However, its commitment to black members left much to be desired. Few within the UAW's leadership were black, and the union did little to compel the companies not to discriminate against black workers. DRUM and other Revolutionary Union Movement offshoots picketed UAW headquarters and also began to agitate for a radical redress of black grievances in the larger community.[48]

With respect to social policies, a narrow class-first approach will be similarly unable to dismantle racist and patriarchal structures. Rather than abolish the horrendously racist U.S. prison system, the class-firsters propose a full-employment program, with guaranteed public jobs if the private sector cannot generate enough work. The eradication of the criminal "injustice" system would be divisive within the working class, they say. A full-employment guarantee, by contrast, would have a more general appeal and would benefit minority workers because they have much higher unemployment rates. A similar case can be made for national health insurance or low-cost public housing. Fight for what unites the working class not what might divide it. Unfortunately, however, these class-based plans will not close the gap between the wages of black and white employees, unless they are combined with affirmative actions aimed directly at black workers. And if we do not insist that those who have faced brutal discrimination become leaders in all our movements, how will any progressive policy be put into practice that does not primarily benefit those who are already in superior positions, given that these people already dominate so many radical efforts to change the world?[49]

There have been left-wing movements around the world for at least 150 years, and yet racial and gender hierarchies are still with us. Just how powerful these are can be seen in those countries that have had socialist revolutions. In the USSR, there was a sense of gender and sexual liberation afoot after the 1917 revolution.[50] Led in part by the Bolshevik leader Alexandra Kollantai, the new society began to move toward a radical reconceptualization of sexuality and gender, as well as new laws that decriminalized homosexuality, gave full social rights to those living together without marriage, freed women from legal servitude to their husbands, socialized childcare, made divorce routine, legalized abortion, and pioneered a new set of social welfare services provided by the state. Kollantai argued, correctly, "for the necessity of carrying out ideological struggle over the structure of gender and sexual relations simultaneously with the social and economic struggles." For her, these were class issues, which would seem obviously true since it had been women workers and peasants, who by force of their numbers and economically inferior social position were those most adversely affected by the regressive gender relations of Soviet societies before 1917.

Nothing like the liberation of women engendered by the Russian Revolution had ever happened in any country in the world. Yet, by the late 1920s and early 1930s, Joseph Stalin had taken control of the Bolshevik Party and the Soviet state, and all of what Kollantai had fought for was reversed and abandoned. Women did continue to make gains on the economic front; the country needed their labor, and within a few decades, women dominated such formerly male job preserves as medicine and engineering. But even this has been reversed with the demise of the Soviet Union and the resurrection of the reactionary Orthodox Church.

Few countries have made greater strides in combating structural racism than Cuba. Since the revolutionary forces gained control of the country in 1959, laws have been enacted ending all forms of racial discrimination. Efforts have been made to incorporate black Cubans fully and equally into all elements of society, including the Communist Party and the government. Cuba's leading scholar of race, political economist Esteban Morales Domínguez, states: "Cuba is the only country in the world in which blacks and mestizos have the state and the government as their ally. If there had not been a revolution, blacks would have had to make one in order to reach the level that more than a few of us have achieved."[51] He adds ". . . we can argue that the black and mulatto population on the island is the most educated and healthy group of African descendants in this hemisphere, and that no other country has done so much to eliminate racial injustice and discrimination as has Cuba."[52] Cuban military forces in southern Africa were critical to the defeat of apartheid in South Africa and colonialism in Angola. Yet, the ellipsis I placed in the last quote hides the words that begin it: "In spite of the racism that still exists in Cuban society. . ." Especially after the Special Period that commenced with the end of the Soviet Union, which brought with it a focus on foreign tourism as a means to obtain foreign exchange, black Cubans have faced discrimination and inequality. Those suffering most were Afro-Cubans. Cuba is still working hard to address problems of race. But if racial disparities exist there, nearly sixty years after the Revolution and in a society willing to face and deal with this directly, then we can see how important it is to confront the racial hierarchy in whatever working-class struggles come into being.

Ending racial and gender hierarchies is difficult, to say the least.

Think of India with its complex caste system, which combines enormous economic and social injustices that seem particularly immune to solution.[53] There are concrete things that might be done with respect to patriarchy and race. First, women and racial and ethnic groups have built hundreds of organizations and movements to liberate themselves. However, we, especially those of us who are men and white, can support these, we should, but we should also honor their independence and the leadership of those within them. Showing solidarity with oppressed groups is, as David Roediger argues, a harder task than we might imagine.[54] Capital creates differences within labor, and these get embedded in the system as a whole. So, forging alliances among groups with different identities is extremely difficult. Humility and a willingness to thrash out differences might go a long way toward building a unified working-class movement.

Second, in all labor unions and political parties, caucuses of women, racial and ethnic minorities, and LGBT should be encouraged and recognized where they already exist. All working-class organizations should have open spaces for free discussion and debate. The main goal is to address issues directly and forcefully. Don't sweep anything under the rug. Third, as said earlier in this chapter, make combating all the hierarchies within the working class central to the work of organizing, the functioning of every working-class entity, and the building of alternative ways of constructing the production, distribution, and reproduction of society. Mao Zedong said that developing collective relations of production was as important as increasing production, perhaps more so, because only a culture of equality could unleash humanity's creative potential. Fourth, don't allow race and gender hierarchy struggles to be co-opted by mainstream politics. For example, the "Me Too" upsurge has focused mainly on famous men who have assaulted and demeaned women. However, most of the women who daily face male depredations are in the working class. This is where radical efforts should be concentrated, in the workplaces, homes, and communities where most women are exploited and expropriated. In the United States, for example, it is unlikely that top labor leaders are going to press the issue of patriarchy with fervor. Women and male allies should press unions as hard as possible on this. All those who want to change the world should support every anti-racist and anti-patriarchy upheaval.

IMPERIALISM, WITH ITS LAND THEFTS and attendant wars, has caused tens of millions to abandon their homelands and flee to other countries, often in the Global North. These immigrants have suffered every imaginable indignity: forced into squalid camps, robbed by unscrupulous people who "help" them get across border; arrested by border police and kept in detention centers awaiting deportation; compelled to take the worst jobs while living in constant fear of arrest; treated always as second-class persons, even in countries that profess compassion for them.[55] A combination of racism and virulent nationalism has arisen around the world, fueled by neo-fascist political parties, causing still more brutal treatment of immigrants. In the United States, the Trump administration has declared war on immigrants, refusing even asylum requests for women and children in danger of extreme violence in their home countries. It separates parents from children, placing the latter in what amount to thinly disguised concentration camps, run by private enterprises.[56]

Though many protests and other actions supportive of immigrant rights have taken place, labor unions and labor political parties should do much more.[57] They should help fund immigrant rights groups and form their own. They should organize mass demonstrations at camp and detention center sites. They should picket the houses of politicians who have criminalized immigration. Principles of open borders and "No one is illegal" should appear on their banners. They should engage in the immigration education of their members. In the United States, immigrants have been one bright spot in the labor movement, joining unions and engaging is class struggle, whether they are documented or not.[58]

They are far less likely to be criminals or terrorists than the native-born. This is a critically important matter. If the "We" means anything at all, it means embracing immigrants as our brothers and sisters. As a woman from whom we rented an apartment in Tucson said to us about Mexicans coming north, "But they're our neighbors." Indeed, they are.

Direct Action. It takes boldness and courage to attack capital. But attack we must. This system is a human disaster, and it proves itself every day to be incapable of satisfying our most basic needs. It has assaulted all aspects of life, including the metabolism of the earth. If it does not cease to exist, wealth will continue to flow to the top and soon the richest handful of persons will own most of what everyone else depends upon for life. Work will continue to be an exercise in misery. The exhortation to become ever more productive—or else!—will get louder, ringing in our ears until our minds and bodies are shipwrecked. Food supplies will become more contaminated and unfit to eat. Land thefts will accelerate. Rising temperatures will kill us or make us want to kill each other. Authoritarian, neo-fascist governments will become common-place. Barbarism won't be the half of it.

If unions, peasant associations, and political entities are to work together to change the world, to bring an unalienating society into existence, then the motto of Brazil's Landless Workers' Movement must become the rallying cry for everyone: "*Occupy, Resist, Produce.*" Unions must resurrect the strike, which can still cripple production and disrupt the extraction of surplus value from the labor power of the working class. This is especially true in those sectors of the global economy tied together by complex but physically separated supply chains and sophisticated logistics. Railway workers, those who load and unload the giant container ships, sailors and others who work on ships, warehouse employees in the large logistics complexes near the world's large cities, communication workers, IT specialists, call center operators—these are all workers whose efforts keep the flow of goods and services going.

Rolling strikes by teachers, food workers, sanitation employees, on as large a geographical scale as possible, can make capital tremble. Immigrants everywhere around the globe, those who plant and harvest crops, clean houses and hotel rooms, tend the lines in restaurant kitchens, build the houses, do the yard work, take care of people's plumbing, electrical, and mechanical needs, manicure hands and feet, and care for other people's children, can strike, showing both their power and their indispensability and demanding that they be respected. One reason why unions must be democratic, with radical aims, is that they are much more likely to strike, picket (not just workplaces but the homes of their bosses, suppliers, and buyers), and boycott. And when they do, these will be effective because the members have taken control of their actions. The history of strikes tells us this is so. Workers shouldn't have to relearn this history, but if they do, they and society will be rewarded.[59]

Rather than waste time voting for traditional political parties, believing that they can be pressured to the left, workers must confront the state directly. Neoliberalism had ravaged Argentina's working class, exacerbated by an economic collapse that began in 2001, and left much of the workforce unemployed or forced to labor in the informal economy. Traditional labor unions and political institutions, embedded in a corporatist, capital-labor compromise, were no longer relevant to those left behind. To organize themselves, unemployed workers and their allies began to blockade local, regional, and national roads. They came to be known as *piqueteros*, the Spanish word for "picketers." They found that they could stall commerce and, in this way, stop the flow of profits just like wage workers do when they strike. Many groups were formed, some community-based, democratic, with informal education of members, and sometimes they attempted to produce goods and services. Although the participants eventually succumbed to internal disagreements among the left-wing parties that infiltrated them, government repression and concession, and exhaustion, they provide another example of the kind of organization that foreshadows a better future.[60]

Members of the Movement for Black Lives have taken to the streets of U.S. towns and cities for several years now, protesting continuing police violence against black men, women, and children. In September 2017, protestors blocked streets in St. Louis to demand justice in yet another acquittal of a police murderer. Such actions, combined with a growing and sophisticated movement aimed at black liberation, not only empower participants but make visible in a direct way the realities of black lives in the United States. Actions give witness, and they force the state to respond, either with further violence or concession. Combined with lawsuits, and in some places attempts to organize production, these actions eschew ordinary politics and attack capital and state directly. In Greensboro, North Carolina, activists in the black community, following in the footsteps of Occupy Wall Street, made a valiant effort to gain ownership of an abandoned shopping mall, with the goal of starting a group of worker-community cooperatives, including a grocery store. Many such efforts fail, like the Argentine *piqueteros* did, but they serve a radical educational function and provide a base upon which to build future forms of collective self-help and confrontation.[61] In an important sense, these actions reflect the heritage of the Black Panther Party, which took seriously a duty to occupy, resist, and produce. The party initiated a remarkable number of collective self-help measures, all of which provided services that poor communities could not get in the capitalist marketplace. "These programs eventually included the Free Breakfast for Children Program, liberation schools, free health clinics, the Free Food Distribution Program, the Free Clothing Program, child development centers, the Free Shoe Program, the Free Busing to Prison Program, the Sickle Cell Anemia Research Foundation, free housing cooperatives, the Free Pest Control Program, the Free Plumbing and Maintenance Program, renter's assistance, legal aid, the Seniors Escorts Program, and the Free Ambulance Program."[62]

Occupation is a direct action that can take various forms, but it typically involves efforts to retake the commons or convert private property into common property. Occupy Wall Street is a famous example. Beginning in Zuccotti Park in the Wall Street district of New York, in September 2011, it spread throughout the United States and the world.

> Public spaces were occupied; clashes with police ensued immediately; diverse discussions and debates took place; the movement spread rapidly across the nation and then the world; and millions of people were energized and made to feel part of something of great importance. Open-air classrooms scrutinized critical issues. People learned that they could make decisions and effectively organize daily life. Those camped out in Zuccotti secured food and shelter, took care of sanitation, and solved complex problems of logistics every day.[63]

Homeless people can occupy abandoned buildings or set up tent encampments in public spaces. Community groups can take over abandoned land for gardens. Workers can occupy closed factories. The act of occupation can lead to an arrangement with government authorities for the sale of the property at a nominal price or one in which the state turns a blind eye to the occupation. Again, we can have collective self-help at work.

We have seen in the case of Cuban agriculture that the state can encourage and support working-class cooperation. To a lesser degree, this has been true in Venezuela as well. Even before Hugo Chávez became president, there were local associations in both rural and urban areas that had begun to hold meetings of the people in a neighborhood or small geographical area to discuss common problems and their solutions. Chávez saw that such groups could be the foundation of a participatory socialism in which control over society could eventually devolve to the working class, replacing the liberal democratic state that had proven itself incapable of meeting basic social needs. Thus were born the communal councils, of which there are now 47,000 in the country:

A communal council is the assembly of a self-chosen territory. In urban areas it comprises 150–200 families or living units, in rural areas 20–30 and in indigenous areas, that are even less densely populated, 10–20, and they decide themselves what is the territory of the community. The communal council is the assembly of all people of the community that decides on all matters.

The communal councils form workgroups for different issues, depending on their needs: infrastructure, water, sports, culture, etc., and these workgroups elaborate proposals that are then voted by the community assembly to establish what is more important. Then they get the projects financed through public institutions. The financing structure that was created was no longer attached to the representative institutions at a local level, which would have brought them into this direct, unequal competition. . . . Instead it was situated at a national or at least regional level. And this created a possibility to have a more community-centered, more independent . . . decision-making.[64]

Funded projects have generated community-controlled enterprises, which can supply goods and services locally, be exchanged with similar entities in nearby territories, or sold in the marketplace. There are also some 6,000 communes, which combine several councils and coordinate activities at a larger spatial level. There are difficulties of unequal power between councils and communes, and between both of these and the state. They have been worsened by the economic crisis and attempts by U.S. imperialism to overthrow the Venezuela government. At the national level, the government, following Chávez's analytical framework, has relied too much on the belief that oil revenues and the material wealth that these generated would allow socialism at the base of society to outstrip the capitalism that still dominated the overall economy. The terrible economic crisis now gripping the nation has shown the error in this way of thinking and acting. Hopefully, however, the ideological climate in both councils and communes has been one in which the "We" has taken hold, weakening the grip of the "I" on people's consciousness. Even with the turmoil engulfing Venezuela now (June 2018), this shift in thinking might make it difficult to overturn the positive steps that have been undertaken.[65] With both council and commune, as well as several attempts at worker control of factories, the working class, which, as always, includes peasants, we see an expansion of the commons, an assertion by those whose lives have been severely circumscribed by capital to take back what should have been theirs to begin with.[66]

Control of land has been a recurring theme among black dissidents. The Nation of Islam has farms in various parts of the United States that produce organic food. Some in the U.S. Communist Party argued that the "Black Belt" running across the southern United States constituted a nation that should be independent of the nation that had enslaved black people. The Black Panther Party and Malcolm X stressed the need to control this most important means of production. To produce necessary goods, land is required. Without it, how can any group be economically independent? Another example of the logic of "occupy, resist, produce" has been taking place in the U.S. city of Jackson, Mississippi, and the surrounding area.[67] The movement in Jackson is called Cooperation Jackson (CJ), and it grew out of various efforts by blacks to build a socialist community in the heart of U.S. capitalism. The rallying cry of the people who began Cooperation Jackson—one of the most notable of these was black radical Chokwe Lumumba, who eventually became Jackson's mayor, something remarkable in its own right—was "Free the Land." After doing some preliminary organizing in the area, they acquired land and began to develop an ambitious plan of eco-socialist production, distribution, and education. In the South, global warming is going to inundate low-lying areas with water. This fact and the disaster in New Orleans after Hurricane Katrina made these leaders grasp that any scheme that doesn't take ecology seriously cannot hope to change the world. Therefore, CJ maintained from the beginning that whatever they did had to be based upon the principle of sustaining the environment.

The CJ project has four goals: gaining black working-class control of the means of production in Jackson and the area close to it; building and advancing the development of the ecologically regenerative forces of production; making the working class the agent of combining the means of production into socially useful outputs; and democratically transforming Jackson, and then the state of Mississippi, and outward to the entire South. CJ has started cooperatives, a cooperative school, training center, union, and bank. Farms and grocery stores are an integral part of cooperative production. There is much more to CJ, including the use of technologies like 3D printers to make useful goods, the development of substantive political democracy, and eco-friendly public infrastructure. The industrialization plan is particularly ambitious. It can be criticized as not feasible, but in any conceivable future, goods will have to be made using one technology or another. CJ, by beginning to conceptualize this and then implementing it, will help show the way forward.

In all the examples in this section, education has been of paramount importance. Experts and novices learn from one another in non-hierarchical, collective settings. As stated near the beginning of this chapter, radical education will be critical for the struggle to terminate the rule of capital and build a different world. There has been heated discussion recently about higher education in the United States, as racial and ethnic minorities, and especially women, have sought to pressure colleges and universities to become more inclusive. There is much to applaud in these efforts, but as historian Robin Kelley points out, the university cannot be reformed by the simple addition of more black, brown, and women teachers and students, more diversity training, and safe spaces. Institutions of higher learning are integral to the reproduction of capitalism and its multiple oppressions. It is possible to learn in them, but this learning should be used to subvert the colleges themselves, to supersede them. Take from these institutions what they offer and then build alternative forms of education in spaces controlled by the working class.[68]

With respect to labor education, working-class political parties and organizations began labor colleges in the first forty years of the twentieth century. I wrote a five-part essay on radical labor education, in which I provided some of the history:

> In the United States, the Communist Party (CPUSA) began the New York Workers School in 1923 (later renamed the Jefferson School) and remained active in worker education until the Cold War assault on the left. The CPUSA also had schools throughout the country, including the California Labor School in the Bay Area. These saw as their purpose the development of a radical class consciousness among workers, and they tried to link theoretical knowledge of capitalism with practical efforts to construct a radical working-class culture. They conducted hundreds of classes for thousands of students, especially during and after the Second World War. The curriculum centered around Marxism, which was called the "science of society," but around this center there were courses on every imaginable subject: literature, art, drama, psychology, even dressing for success (this last had a class focus, aimed at both women who would be participating in their unions as leaders and immigrants and their children, who needed to know the norms of their new country). Many of the instructors were top-notch scholars and artists. Dashiell Hammett taught a course on the mystery novel, for instance. All of the Party's schools were connected in one way or another to the labor movement, mainly to the left-led unions of the Congress of Industrial Organizations (CIO), some of whose leaders were either Party members or "fellow travelers."
>
> There were other schools for worker education, for example the Brookwood Labor College, Work People's College, and the Highlander Folk School. All aimed to prepare workers for struggle, in their trade unions and in the larger society. Willing to ally themselves with supportive unions and nonsectarian in their admissions practices, they were committed to a radically liberal education. Interestingly, Local 189 of the Communication

Workers of America, a contemporary union of labor educators (today, after a merger with the University and College Labor Education Association, it is the United Association for Labor Education or UALE), began as Local 189 of the American Federation of Teachers, which represented the faculty at Brookwood Labor College. Work People's College was begun by Finnish immigrants in Minnesota and later came under the sway of the Industrial Workers of the World (IWW), which reopened the school in 2006. The Highlander Folk School is the most famous of these colleges, and it is still going strong as the Highlander Research and Education Center. One of its most famous students was Rosa Parks.[69]

Robin Kelley gives several examples of black Americans educating themselves, not only about their oppression but about their rejection of and battles to end it and forge a better world. The Mississippi Freedom Schools of the early 1960s, whose students and teachers "didn't want equal opportunity in a burning house; they wanted to build a new house." The black women of Mt. Vernon, New York, who began an education program a few years later, "saw education as a vehicle for collective transformation and an incubator of knowledge, not a path to upward mobility and material wealth." There have been independent black schools and institutes and numerous study groups started without much money but with a desire, as Kelley puts it, to "love, study, struggle."[70]

FINAL WORDS

The unstated implication of everything said in this book is that the working class *must* change the world. There is really no choice. The long rule of capital has created profoundly alienated conditions for nearly all of humanity. Despite the creation of unimaginable quantities of goods and services, capitalism has never managed to ensure that these are distributed with even a tolerable degree of inequality. Today, the combined wealth of eight billionaires is as great as the total wealth of half the people in the world.[71] After several hundred years, there are still several billion people existing on the brink of economic ruin. Work is still hell for all but a few. Today it is a rare person who has not lived through a war; and the greatest imperial power, the United States, is waging war in scores of countries and has subjected several to absolute ruin. Capital has even managed to upend Earth's metabolism, generating manifold disasters that might soon make our planet largely uninhabitable. If we are to somehow recover our humanness and reverse course, the working class will *have* to change the world. Capital will never do it, nor will the relatively well-off middle class of small-scale businesspersons and professionals, who are more likely to support fascism than profound social change. Only the working class, with its vast numbers and potential power, can get the job done.

Here in this last chapter, I have offered some ideas as to how the world can begin anew. My argument can be summed up in a few words. Only radical thinking and acting have any chance of staving off accelerating levels of barbarism. Newer instruments must be forged: radically democratic labor unions and political parties, a scaling-up of collective self-help activities, massive levels of "occupy, resist, produce." The old ways have failed: traditional labor unions and social democratic politics are now irrelevant in that they will never bring about radical social transformation. So too are mainstream environmental groups, the non-governmental organizations that have proliferated like invasive species, and the plethora of liberal feminist and ethnic and racial advocacy associations. Their stakes are tied to the bourgeois order of things; mainly they want just a slightly larger share of the pie. What the pie is and how it came to be are matters that sail over their heads in terms of understanding.

We cannot afford to settle for incremental changes that, even if they happen, never amount to what is qualitatively and radically different, and can soon enough be reversed and usually are. To believe otherwise is surely utopian. It is the radical upending of the social order that is now hardheaded realism, the only path forward. No doubt, it might already be too late. It will take time for a class riven with so many fundamental cleavages, by race/ethnicity, gender, and imperialism most importantly, to unify itself and destroy its class enemy. Mother Earth may take her revenge on us before that. In the meantime, though, best to do what we can, in whatever ways of which we are capable: by any and all tactics, everywhere, all the time, in every part of the capitalist system. Fight landlords, disrupt classrooms, take on bosses, write, nothing is unimportant. And as we do this, remember that those who have suffered the most—workers and peasants in the Global South, minorities in the Global North, working-class women everywhere—are going to lead struggles or they are likely to fail. Speaking of his native India, the revolutionary, Bhagat Singh, who was executed by the British colonialists in 1931 when he was twenty-three years old, said something still true: "The real revolutionary armies are in the villages and in factories, the peasantry and the labourers."[72] With humility, I offer them my solidarity. I hope we all do.

Notes

1. The Working Class

1. Julia Wallace and Tatiana Cozzarelli, "Cop Organizers Aren't Comrades," http://www.leftvoice.org/Cop-Organizers-Aren-t-Comrades.

2. An excellent book on the changing composition of the U.S. labor force is Kim Moody, *On New Terrain: How Capital Is Reshaping the Battleground of Class War* (Chicago: Haymarket Books, 2017), Kindle edition. On the changing positions of physicians, see Howard Waitzkin, "Disobedience: Doctor Workers, Unite!," in Howard Waitzkin and the Working Group on Health Beyond Capitalism, *Health Care Under the Knife: Moving Beyond Capitalism for Our Health* (New York: Monthly Review Press, 2018).

3. For examples of intern labor, see https://www.vice.com/en_us/article/mv5ekb/the-exploited-laborers-of-the-liberal-media.

4. Samir Amin, "World Poverty, Pauperization and Capital Accumulation," *Monthly Review* 55/5 (October 2003): 1; La Via Campesina, *Declaration of Rights of Peasants—Women and Men*, 2009, https://viacampesina.net/downloads/PDF/EN-3.pdf.

5. See Baba Umar, "India's Shocking Farmer Suicide Epidemic," *Al Jazeera*, May 18, 2015, https://www.aljazeera.com/indepth/features/2015/05/india-shocking-farmer-suicide-epidemic-150513121717412.html. Global warming, itself the result of capital's unquenchable thirst for profits, may also be contributing to the suicides. See Michael Safi, "Suicides of nearly 60,000 Indian Farmers Linked to Climate Change, Study Claims," *The Guardian*, July 31, 2017, https://www.theguardian.com/

environment/2l017/jul/31/suicides-of-nearly-60000-indian-farmers-linked-to-climate-change-study-claims.

6.   Bernard D'Mello, *India After Naxalbari: Unfinished History* (New York: Monthly Review Press, 2018).

7.   The classic work is Edgar Snow's *Red Star Over China* (New York: Random House, 1937).

8.   V. I. Lenin, "The Proletariat and the Peasantry," in *Lenin: Collected Works*, vol. 8 (Moscow: Foreign Languages Publishing House, 1962), 231–36.

9.   This is a theme of Zhun Xu's *From Commune to Capitalism* (New York: Monthly Review Press, 2018).

10. See Michael Schulman, "Is China Stealing Jobs? It May Be Losing Them, Instead," *New York Times*, July 22, 2016, https://www.nytimes.com/2016/07/23/business/international/china-jobs-donald-trump.html; Indermit Gill, "Future Development Reads: China's Shifting Manufacturing Labor Pool Is Creating Global Dreams—And Nightmares," Brookings Institution, November 17, 2017, https://www.brookings.edu/blog/future-development/2017/11/17/future-development-reads-the-manufacturing-dreams-and-nightmares-of-china/.

11. Mike Davis, *Planet of Slums* (New York: Verso, 2006).

12. Martha Allen Chen, *The Informal Economy: Definitions, Theories and Policies* (Cambridge, MA: Women in Informal Employment: Globalizing and Organizing [WIEGO], 2012), http://www.wiego.org/sites/wiego.org/files/publications/files/Chen_WIEGO_WP1.pdf.

13. For background on the New York Taxi Workers Alliance, see http://www.nytwa.org.

14. Ursula Huws, "The Underpinnings of Class in the Digital Age: Living, Labour and Value," in *Registering Class: Socialist Register,* ed. Leo Panitch and Vivek Chibber (New York: Monthly Review Press, 2014), 80–107, see esp. the chart on 84, though the entire article is well worth reading.

15. The data in this section are taken from the ILO website and from the WESO report. The global population number can be found at http://www.worldometers.info/world-population/. The report can be downloaded at http://www.ilo.org; click on the Publications tab.

16. John Bellamy Foster, Robert W. McChesney, and R. Jamil Jonna, "The Global Reserve Army of Labor and the New Imperialism," *Monthly Review* 63/6 (November 2011): 1–31.

17. Michael D. Yates, *The Great Inequality* (London: Routledge, 2016), Kindle edition.

18. These data are taken from the useful and informative website of the World Prison Brief, at http://www.prisonstudies.org.

19. My calculation is based upon data in http://www.ilo.org/wcmsp5/ groups/public/@dgreports/@dcomm/documents/publication/ wcms_575499.pdf. There are 44 million children working in services and industry. Those between five and fifteen years old (the ILO counts children between five and seventeen as child laborers) account for 75 percent of all child laborers; 75 percent of 44 million is 33 million.

20. For some data on peasants, see https://newint.org/blog/2017/12/14/ peasants-feed-world.

21. For some data on the number of peasants, see https://www.the-guardian.com/global-development/poverty-matters/2011/apr/18/ international-day-peasants-rights-grow-food.

22. See ILO website, www.ilo.org.

23. For labor force data, see https://www.dol.gov/wb/factsheets/qf-labor-force-10.htm; https://www.dol.gov/wb/factsheets/qf-laborforce-10.htm.

24. For a breakdown of the global labor force by sector, see http://www.ilo. org/ilostat.

25. UNFPA, *Worlds Apart: Reproductive Health and Rights in an Age of Inequality*, 2017, 46, https://www.unfpa.org/swop.

26. An informative summary of the UNFPA report is Rachael Revesz, "Women Around the World Earn a Quarter Less than Men, Finds UN Report," *Independent*, October 17, 2017, http://www.independent. co.uk/news/world/women-salaries-men-gender-pay-gap-world-un-report-a8005796.html.

27. The data that follow are taken from Yates, *The Great Inequality*.

28. Ibid., citing a report from the Economic Policy Institute, http://epi.org/ page/-/BriefingPaper288.pdf.

29. Yates, *The Great Inequality*, Kindle edition.

30. For unemployment in South Africa, see "White versus Black Unemployment in South Africa," *Business Tech*, https://businesstech.co.za/ news/general/96887/white-vs-black-unemployment-in-south -africa/.

31. It would require a monumental bibliography to cite even a small percentage of articles and books that document these various forms of discrimination, but several will give readers examples of the economic and social gaps marking those who face discrimination: Jie Zong and Jeanne Batalova, "Mexican Immigrants in the United States," Migration Policy Institute, March 17, 2016, https://www.migrationpolicy.org/arti-cle/mexican-immigrants-united-states; World Bank Policy Brief, "Still Among the Poorest of the Poor," 2011, http://siteresources.worldbank. org/EXTINDPEOPLE/Resources/407801-1271860301656/HDNEN_ indigenous_clean_0421.pdf; Ram Puniyani, "Muslims in India: Appeasement or Discrimination," *The Companion*, January 25, 2018, http://thecompanion.in/muslims-india-appeasement-discrimination/.

32. See https://www.bls.gov/opub/reports/minimum-wage/2016/home.htm.
33. ILO, *Global Wage Report, 2016/17*, http://www.ilo.org/wcmsp5/groups/public/—dgreports/—dcomm/—publ/documents/publication/wcms_537846.pdf.
34. See https://www.statista.com/statistics/226956/average-world-wages-in-purchasing -power-parity-dollars/.
35. Cited in Yates, *The Great Inequality*.
36. Franz Fanon, *The Wretched of the Earth* (New York: Grove Press, 1963).
37. E. V. Debs, "Statement to the Court," September 18, 1918, https://www.marxists.org/archive/debs/works/1918/court.htm.
38. See http://www.worldometers.info/world-population/, 20.
39. See http://highroadforhumanrights.org/wp-content/uploads/2011/02/Indias-Shame-The-Nation2.pdf.
40. Jonathan Silvers, "Child Labor in Pakistan," *The Atlantic*, February 1996, http://theatlantic.com/magazine/archive/1996/02/child-labor -in-pakistan/304660/.
41. See https://www.asbestos.com/occupations/construction-workers/.
42. See http://www.wiego.org/informal-economy/occupational-groups/construction-workers.
43. See http://dbacon.igc.org/Work/03AsbestosRevolt.htm.
44. See https://cleanclothes.org/resources/publications/factsheets/general-factsheet-garment-industry-february-2015.pdf; http://www.wiego.org/informal-economy/occupational-groups/garment-workers.
45. John Smith, *Imperialism in the Twenty-First Century* (New York: Monthly Review Press, 2016), 9.
46. See http://www.industriall-union.org/report-electronics-industry-organizing-and-fighting-against-precarious-work; https://www.thenation.com/article/high-tech-manufacturings-disposable-workers/.
47. On Foxconn, see https://www.theguardian.com/technology/2017/jun/18/foxconn-life-death-forbidden-city-longhua-suicide-apple-iphone-brian-merchant-one-device-extract. Merchant's book was published by Bantam Press (London) in 2017.
48. The data are for 2017. See http://www.ilo.org/ilostat/.
49. David Bacon, "Child Labor: The Hidden History of Mexico's Export Farms," http://dbacon.igc.org/Mexico/03Onions.htm. The excerpt in the text has taken several sentences from David Bacon's essay and reordered them to make the excerpt coherent.
50. This number is taken from Bureau of Labor Statistics data: https://www.bls.gov/emp/ep_table_201.htm.
51. Moody, *On New Terrain*.
52. Ibid.

53. Michael D. Yates, "Work Is Hell," *Counterpunch*, May 20, 2009, https://www.counterpunch.org/2009/05/20/work-is-hell/.

54. See https://www.bls.gov/emp/ep_table_104.htm.

55. Yates, *The Great Inequality*.

56. Soutik Biswas, "Why Are India's Housewives Killing Themselves?," BBC News, April 12, 2016, http://www.bbc.com/news/world-asia-india-35994601.

2. Some Theoretical Considerations

1. See the 2014 report by the International Labour Office: http://www.ilo.org/wcmsp5/groups/public/—ed_norm/—declaration/documents/publication/wcms_243The Working D391.pdf.

2. Marc Dowie, "Pinto Madness," *Mother Jones*, September–October 1977, http://www.motherjones.com/politics/1977/09/pinto-madness/#.

3. For a bonanza of wealth statistics, see http://publications.credit-suisse.com/tasks/render/file/index.cfm?fileid=12DFFD63-07D1-EC63-A3D5F67356880EF3.

4. This quote is taken from https://inequality.org/wp-content/uploads/2017/11/BILLIONAIRE-BONANZA-2017-Embargoed.pdf.

5. Karl Marx, *Capital: A Critique of Political Economy*, vol. 1 (London: Penguin, 2004), Kindle edition.

6. For an analysis of the modern intensification of work, see Kim Moody, *On New Terrain: How Capital Is Reshaping the Battleground of Class War* (Chicago: Haymarket Books, 2017), Kindle edition.

7. Bruce Nelson, *Workers on the Waterfront: Seamen, Longshoremen, and Unionism in the 1930s* (Champaign: University of Illinois Press, 1990).

8. On CWA solidarity, see https://www.cwa-union.org/national-issues/international-solidarity/international-solidarity-cwa; http://tnlabour.in/automobile-industry/5156.

9. Harry Braverman, *Labor and Monopoly Capital* (New York: Monthly Review Press, 1974), 127–62.

10. Natalie Kitroeff and Geoffrey Mohan, "Wages rise on California farms. Americans still don't want the job," *Los Angeles Times*, http://www.latimes.com/projects/la-fi-farms-immigration/#nt=featured-content.

11. See Carlos Salas, Bruce Campbell, and Robert E. Scott, "NAFTA at Seven," June 6, 2001, http://www.epi.org/publication/briefingpapers_nafta01_ca/.

12. On this draconian measure, see E. P. Thompson, *Whigs and Hunters: The Origins of the Black Act* (New York: Pantheon, 1975).

13. Marx, *Capital* 1:874. On page 873, Marx refers to an elite that were, according to the creation myth of capitalism, "diligent, intelligent and above all frugal."

14. Theodore W. Allen, *The Invention of the White Race*, Vol. 1 (New York: Verso, 2012; David R. Roediger, *The Wages of Whiteness: Race and the Making of the American Working Class* (New York: Verso, 1991).

15. Robin D. G. Kelley, *Hammer and Hoe: Alabama Communists During the Great Depression* (Chapel Hill: University of North Carolina Press, 1990), Kindle edition.

16. On modern imperialism, see Harry Magdoff, *Imperialism Without Colonies* (New York: Monthly Review Press, 2003); Harry Magdoff, *Imperialism: From the Colonial Era to the Present* (New York: Monthly Review Press, 1978): and John Smith, *Imperialism in the Twenty-First Century: Globalization, Super-Exploitation, and Capitalism's Final Crisis:* (New York: Monthly Review Press, 2016).

17. Bernard D'Mello, *India after Naxalbari: Unfinished History* (New York: Monthly Review Press, 2018).

18. Nancy Fraser, "Behind Marx's Hidden Abode: For an Expanded Conception of Capitalism," *New Left Review* 86 (March–April 2014): 61.

19. Julia Puscheck, "Women and Propaganda in America During World War II: Methods in which the United States Propaganda Organizations Targeted Various Age Groups of Women," June 8, 2010, http://digitalcommons.calpoly.edu/cgi/viewcontent.cgi?article=1013&context=histsp.

20. Kohei Saito, *Karl Marx's Ecosocialism: Capital, Nature, and the Unfinished Critique of Political Economy* (New York: Monthly Review Press, 2017), 245–47.

21. John Bellamy Foster and Brett Clark, "The Expropriation of Nature," *Monthly Review* 69/10 (March 2018): 1–27.

22. Oliver Milman, "'It's wrong to stink up other people's lives': Fighting the Manure Lagoons of North Carolina," *The Guardian*, May 24, 2018, https://www.theguardian.com/environment/2018/may/24/pig-farm -agriculture-its-wrong-to-stink-up-other-peoples-lives-fighting-the- manure-lagoons-of-north-carolina.

23. Michael D. Yates, "Let's Get Serious About Inequality and Socialism," April 30, 2016, *Truthout*, http://www.truth-out.org/opinion/ item/35841-let-s-get-serious-about-inequality-and-socialism; Michael D. Yates, "Bernie Sanders' 'Political Revolution' Reconsidered," *Counterpunch*, March 2, 2016, https://www.counterpunch.org/2016/03/ 02/bernie-sanderss-political-revolution-reconsidered/.

24. See Adrian Pabst, "Henry VIII and the Birth of Capitalism," *The Guardian*, May 1, 2009, https://www.theguardian.com/commentisfree/ belief/2009/may/01/religion-henry-vii-monasteries; Perry Anderson, *Lineages of the Absolutist State* (London: Verso, 1979); Michael Tigar,

Law and the Rise of Capitalism (New York: Monthly Review Press, 2000); Richard Rothstein, *The Color of Law: A Forgotten History of How Our Government Segregated America* (New York: W. W. Norton, 2018); István Mészáros, "Preface to Beyond Leviathan," *Monthly Review* 69/ 9 (February 2018): 47–57.

25. Alejandro Reuss, *The General Theory and the Current Crisis: A Primer on Keynes' Economics* (Boston: Dollars & Sense, 2013), available at http://www.dollarsandsense.org/archives/2013/1013reusskeynespar tIV.html.

26. On U.S. labor law, see Michael D. Yates, *Power on the Job* (Boston: South End Press, 1994).

27. Karl Marx and Frederick Engels, *Manifesto of the Communist Party*, 15.

28. Martin Gilens and Benjamin I. Page, "Testing Theories of American Politics: Elites, Interest Groups, and Average Citizens," *Perspectives on Politics* 12/3 (September 2013): 564–81. For a useful summary of the collusion between capital and the state in the United States, including the power business now exerts over all levels of government (federal, state, and local), see Kim Moody, *On New Terrain* (London: Verso, 2017). Kindle edition.

29. John Bellamy Foster, *Trump in the White House: Tragedy and Farce* (New York: Monthly Review Press, 2017).

30. Samuel Bowles and Herbert Gintis, *Schooling in Capitalist America: Educational Reform and the Contradictions of Economic Life* (New York: Basic Books, 1976); Henry Giroux, *America's Education Deficit and the War on Youth* (New York: Monthly Review Press, 2013). On contemporary struggles over schooling, see Howard Ryan, *Educational Justice: Teaching and Organizing Against the Corporate Juggernaut* (New York: Monthly Review Press, 2016).

31. John Marsh, *Class Dismissed: Why We Cannot Teach or Learn Our Way Out of Inequality* (New York: Monthly Review Press, 2011); Gerald Coles, *Miseducating for the Global Economy: How Corporate Power Damages Education and Subverts Students' Futures* (New York: Monthly Review Press, 2018).

32. The classic study is Edward S. Herman and Noam Chomsky, *Manufacturing Consent: The Political Economy of the Mass Media* (New York: Pantheon Books, 1988).

33. For Cuba, see Salim Lamrani, *The Economic War Against Cuba: A Historical and Legal Perspective on the U.S. Blockade* (New York: Monthly Review Press, 2013); and Salim Lamrani, *Cuba, the Media, and the Challenge of Impartiality* (New York: Monthly Review Press, 2014). On the Soviet Union, see Jeremy Kuzmarov and John Marciano, *The Russians Are Coming, Again: The First Cold War as Tragedy, the Second*

as Farce (New York: Monthly Review Press, 2018). On Venezuela, see Richard Seymour, "A Review of U.S. Media Coverage on Venezuela," https://www.telesurtv.net/english/opinion/A-Review-of-US-Media-Coverage-on-Venezuela-20170824-0022.html.

34.   Some web news providers, such as The Daily Beast, are now unionized, and this has helped journalists earn more money.

3. Nothing to Lose but Their Chains

1.   Karl Marx and Frederick Engels, *Manifesto of the Communist Party*, in *Marx/Engels Selected Works*, vol. 1 (Moscow: Progress Publishers, 1969).

2.   It should be noted that feudal entities existed long into at least the nineteenth century—for example, large agricultural estates in Latin America—and these operated much like slavery, though probably not without the same drive to accumulate capital as slave plantations in the United States.

3.   Harry Braverman, *Labor and Monopoly Capital: The Degradation of Work in the Twentieth Century* (New York: Monthly Review Press, 1998), Kindle edition.

4.   Charles Babbage, *On the Economy of Machinery and Manufactures*, 4th ed. (London: Charles Knight, 1835).

5.   Braverman, *Labor and Monopoly Capital*, 54–57.

6.   Ibid., 146–53.

7.   On bread riots in Tewkesbury, England, see Derek Benson, "The Tewkesbury Bread Riot of 1795," *Bristol Radical History Group*, 2013, https://www.brh.org.uk/site/articles/the-tewkesbury-bread-riot-of-1795/.

8.   For a list of food riots, see https://en.wikipedia.org/wiki/List_of_food_riots.

9.   Marcus Rediker and Peter Linebaugh, "The Many-Headed Hydra: Sailors, Slaves, and the Atlantic Working Class in the Eighteenth Century," http://onlinelibrary.wiley.com/doi/10.1111/j.1467-6443.1990.tb00149.x/pdf.

10.   E. P. Thompson, *The Making of the English Working Class* (New York: Open Road Media, 2016), Kindle edition.

11.   Ibid.

12.   For examples, see https://www.marxists.org/archive/marx/works/1864/iwma/index.htm.

13.   For the IWW preamble, see https://www.iww.org/culture/official/preamble.shtml.

14.   The AFL was founded in 1886. The quotation is from the first paragraph, which is replicated in the 1912 version: https://babel.hathitrust.

org/cgi/pt?id=uiug.30112081492636;view=1up;seq=6.

15. For Russia, see Paul LeBlanc, *October Song* (Chicago: Haymarket Books, 2017); for Cuba, see Steve Cushion, *A Hidden History of the Cuban Revolution: How the Working Class Shaped the Guerrillas' Victory* (New York: Monthly Review Press, 2016).

16. Karl Marx, *Critique of the Gotha Program*, 1875, https://www.marxists.org/archive/marx/works/1875/gotha/.

17. Adam Smith, *An Inquiry into the Nature and Causes of the Wealth of Nations* (New York: Modern Library, 1937), 734–35.

18. Ben Hamper, *Rivethead: Tales from the Assembly Line* (New York: Warner Books, 1991), 2.

19. For the gruesome details of orphan labor in British factories, see the novel by Glyn Rose, *The Rape of the Rose* (New York: Simon & Schuster, 1993).

20. Dan Clawson, *Bureaucracy and the Labor Process: The Transformation of U.S. Industry 1860–1920* (New York: Monthly Review Press, 1980).

21. See David Noble, *Forces of Production; A Social History of Industrial Automation* (New York: Knopf, 1984).

22. See the seminal work of John Smith, *Imperialism in the Twenty-First Century: Globalization, Super-Exploitation, and Capitalism's Final Crisis* (New York: Monthly Review Press, 2016).

23. Karl Marx, *Capital: A Critique of Political Economy*, vol. 1 (London: Penguin, 2004), Kindle edition.

24. Michael D. Yates, "Workers of All Countries, Unite: Will This Include the U.S. Labor Movement?" *Monthly Review* 52/3 (July–August 2000): 48.

25. Ibid.

26. See, among many others, David R. Roediger, *Class, Race, and Marxism* (New York: Verso, 2017); W. E. B. Du Bois, *Black Reconstruction in America* (Oxford: Oxford University Press, 2007); Gerald Horne, *The Apocalypse of Settler Colonialism* (New York: Monthly Review Press, 2018); Peter James Hudson, "The Racist Dawn of Capitalism," *Boston Review*, March 14, 2016, http://bostonreview.net/race/robin-d-g-kelley-coates-and-west-jackson; Robin D. G. Kelley, "What Is Racial Capitalism and Why Does It Matter?," lecture given at the University of Washington, November 7, 2017, https://www.youtube.com/watch?v=-gim7W_jQQ; Roxanne Dunbar-Ortiz, *An Indigenous Peoples' History of the United States* (Boston: Beacon Press, 2014); Nancy Fraser, "Expropriation and Exploitation in Racialized Capitalism: A Reply to Michael Dawson," *Critical Historical Studies* 3/1 (Spring 2016): 162–78; Nancy Fraser, "Behind Marx's Hidden Abode: For an Expanded Conception of Capitalism," *New Left Review* 86 (March–April 2014):

55–72; and John Bellamy Foster and Brett Clark, "Women, Nature, and Capital in the Industrial Revolution: A View from Marx," *Monthly Review* 69/8 (January 2018): 1–24.

27. See Theodore W. Allen, *The Invention of the White Race*, vol. 1 (New York: Verso, 2012); Horne, *The Apocalypse of Settler Colonialism*; Walter Johnson, *The River of Dark Dreams: Slavery and Empire in the Cotton Kingdom* (Cambridge, MA: Harvard University Press, 2013).

28. Michael D. Yates, "It's Still Slavery by Another Name," February 23, 2012, http://cheapmotelsandahotplate.org/2012/02/23/slavery-by-another-name/.

29. Fraser, "Behind Marx's Hidden Abode."

30. Two classic studies are Katherine Stone, "The Origin of Job Structures in the Steel Industry," *Review of Radical Political Economics* 6/2 (1974): 113–73; and Stephen A. Marglin, "What Do Bosses Do?: The Origins and Functions of Hierarchy in Capitalist Production," *Review of Radical Political Economics* 6/2 (1974): 60–112.

31. Marx, *Capital*, vol. 1.

32. See Michael D. Yates, "Work Is Hell," in Michael D. Yates, *The Great Inequality* (London: Routledge, 2016), 73–90.

33. Marx's full statement: "In a higher phase of communist society, after the enslaving subordination of the individual to the division of labor, and therewith also the antithesis between mental and physical labor, has vanished; after labor has become not only a means of life but life's prime want; after the productive forces have also increased with the all-around development of the individual, and all the springs of co-operative wealth flow more abundantly—only then can the narrow horizon of bourgeois right be crossed in its entirety and society inscribe on its banners: From each according to his ability, to each according to his needs!" Marx, *Critique of the Gotha Program*.

4. What Hath the Working Class Wrought?

1. The first six paragraphs of this chapter rely heavily on Kunal Chattopadhyay and Soma Marik, "India on Strike," https://www.jaco-binmag.com/2016/10/indian-workers-general-strike; and Anamitra Roychowdhury, "How to Read the 2 September Strike in India?," http://column.global-labour-university.org/2017/06/how-to-read-2-september-strike-in-india.html.

2. Further discussion of the demands and the strike can be found at http://www.industriall-union.org/indian-trade-unions-call-general-strike.

3. For an overview of India's food failures, see Vikas Bajaj, "As Grains Pile Up, India's Poor Still Go Hungry," *New York Times*, June 7, 2012.

4. Aditya Chakrabortty, "Narendra Modi, a man with a massacre on his hands, is not the reasonable choice for India," *The Guardian*, April 7,

2014, https://www.theguardian.com/commentisfree/2014/apr/07/nar-endra -modi-massacre-next-prime-minister-india.

5. Gerald Horne, *Confronting Black Jacobins: The U.S., the Haitian Revolution, and the Origins of the Dominican Republic* (New York: Monthly Review Press, 2015).

6. This number is from the U.S. Bureau of Labor Statistics (BLS). See https://www.bls.gov/news.release/union2.nr0.htm.

7. OECD, *OECD Employment Outlook, 2017* (Paris: OECD Publishing, 2017), 133, http://dx.doi.org/10.1787/empl_outlook-2017-en.

8. As union densities have fallen in the United States, unions' effects on union wages, benefits, inequality, as well as the wages of non-union workers have diminished. In Europe, where densities have fallen but are still higher than in the United States, economic circumstances have not fallen nearly as drastically as in the United States. See Alana Semuels, "Fewer Unions, Lower Pay for Everybody," *The Atlantic*, August 30, 2016, https://www.theatlantic.com/business/archive/2016/08/union-inequality-wages/497954/. See also Lawrence Mishel et al., *The State of Working America*, 12th ed. (Ithaca, NY: Cornell University Press, 2012), 268–79.

9. The most recent study showing that unions reduce inequality is Henry S. Farber et al., "Unions and Inequality Over the Twentieth Century: New Evidence from Survey Data," National Bureau of Economic Research, Working Paper 24587, May 2018. The authors use a detailed data set that allows them to look at the impact of U.S. unions on inequality when unions were strongest, from the late 1930s until the mid-1970s. Their evidence is convincing that unions were the key factor in keeping income inequality in check during this period, reducing it considerably from what it had been in the 1920s and then keeping it roughly constant after that. From the mid-1970s on, as unions diminished in strength, inequality rose. In other words, the relative power of labor compared to capital matters a great deal in terms of how workers fare in capitalist economies. Mainstream economists are oblivious to this and always focus their attention on demand and supply in the marketplace. They miss what Marx said was central: the relations of production. To lessen the impacts of exploitation and expropriation, workers and peasants must struggle for power. The more powerful they are, the weaker capital is.

10. Mishel, *The State of Working America*, 270; Josh Bivens et al., "How Today's Unions Help Working People: Giving Workers the Power to Improve Their Jobs and Unrig the Economy," Economic Policy Institute, August 24, 2017, https://www.epi.org/publication/how-todays-unions-help-working-people-giving-workers-the-power-to-improve-their-jobs-and-unrig-the-economy/.

11. Frank Bardacke, *Trampling Out the Vintage: Cesar Chávez and the Two Souls of the United Farm Workers* (New York: Verso, 2011), 379. For the wage conversion, see https://www.saving.org/inflation/inflation.php?amount=10.

12. http://www.orlandosentinel.com/business/brinkmann-on-business/os-bz-disney-wage-negotiations-20170724-story.html.

13. Mishel, *The State of Working America*, 271.

14. Bivens, "How Today's Unions Help Working People."

15. Ibid.

16. Ibid.

17. Gregg Shotwell, *Autoworkers Under the Gun: A Shop-Floor View of the End of the American Dream* (Chicago: Haymarket Books, 2012), Kindle edition.

18. A good introduction to what unions have done to empower and protect workers is Michael D. Yates, *Why Unions Matter*, 2nd edition (New York: Monthly Review Press, 2009).

19. Tom Wetzel, "Working More Now But Enjoying It Less?," http://ideasandaction.info/2018/03/working-enjoying-less/.

20. Laurie Graham, *On the Line at Subaru-Isuzu: The Japanese Model and the American Worker* (Ithaca, NY: ILR Press, 1995), 74–76.

21. Steve Lohr, "Making Cars the Volvo Way," *New York Times*, June 23, 1987, https://www.nytimes.com/1987/06/23/business/making-cars-the-volvo-way.html.

22. For more on labor education, see Michael D. Yates, "Radical Labor Education, Part 1," http://cheapmotelsandahotplate.org/2010/12/27/radical-labor-education-part-i/. Parts 2 through 5 of this series can be found at the end of Part 1.

23. For labor and politics in the United States, see David Milton, *The Politics of U.S. Labor: From the Great Depression to the New Deal* (New York: Monthly Review Press, 1982); Paul Buhle, *Taking Care of Business: Samuel Gompers, George Meany, Lane Kirkland, and the Tragedy of American Labor* (New York: Monthly Review Press, 1999); Paul Le Blanc, *A Short History of the U.S. Working Class: From Colonial Times to the Twenty-First Century* (Atlantic Highlands, NJ: Humanities Press: 1999); Yates, *Why Unions Matter*.

24. See the *Fight for $15* website at https://fightfor15.org/.

25. The IWW is still in existence and has continued to organize. See https://www.iww.org/history/library/AJMiller/ModernRelevance.

26. For more on syndicalism and anarchism, see Melvin Dubovsky, *We Shall Be All: A History of the Industrial Workers of the World* (New York: Quadrangle Books, 1969); Immanuel Ness, *New Forms of Worker*

Organization: The Syndicalist and Autonomist Restoration of Class-Struggle Unionism (Oakland, CA: PM Press, 2014); Daniel Guerin, *Anarchism: From Theory to Practice* (New York: Monthly Review Press, 1970); David Graeber, *The Democracy Project: A History, a Crisis, a Movement* (New York: Spiegel & Grau, 2013).

27. Wolfgang Abendroth, *A Short History of the European Working Class* (New York: Monthly Review Press, 1972), 63.

28. David Matthews, "The Working-Class Struggle for Welfare in Britain," *Monthly Review* 69/9 (Feburary 2018): 33-45.

29. List based on http://www.crf-usa.org/bill-of-rights-in-action/bria-14-3-c-the -swedish-model-welfare-for-everyone.

30. Bennet Berger and Elena Vaccarino, "Codetermination in Germany—a role model for the UK and the US?," http://bruegel.org/2016/10/codetermination-in-germany-a-role-model-for-the-uk-and-the-us/.

31. Asa Fitch, "Labor Strikes and Worker Protests Erupt Across Iran: 'This Is Slavery,'" *Wall Street Journal*, May 6, 2018, https://www.wsj.com/articles/labor-strikes-and-worker-protests-erupt-across-iran-this-is-slavery-1525626832.

32. AFP, "India's Bidi Workers Suffer for 1,000-a-day Habit," http://www.dailymail.co.uk/wires/afp/article 3045398/Indias-bidi-workers-suffer-1-000-day-habit.html.

33. Debbie Budlander, "Informal Workers and Collective Bargaining: Five Case Studies," WIEGO Organizing Brief No. 9, October 2013, http://www.wiego.org/sites/default/files/publications/files/Budlender-Informal-Workers-Collective-Bargaining-WIEGO-OB9.pdf.

34. Tamás Krausz, "One Hundred Years, One Hundred Messages," *Monthly Review* 69/3 (July-August, 2017): 36.

35. For more on some of the achievements of these revolutions, see Michael A. Lebowitz, *The Contradictions of "Real Socialism": The Conductor and the Conducted* (New York: Monthly Review Press, 2012); Samir Amin, *Russia and the Long Transition from Capitalism to Socialism* (New York: Monthly Review Press, 2016); William Hinton, *Fanshen: A Documentary of Revolution in a Chinese Village* (New York: Monthly Review Press, 2008), first published in 1966; Cliff DuRand, "Cuba's New Cooperatives," *Monthly Review* 69/6 (November 2017): 52–56; Christina Ergas, "Cuban Urban Agriculture as a Strategy for Food Sovereignty," *Monthly Review* 64/19 (March 2013): 46–52.

36. Roger Horowitz, *Negro and White, Unite and Fight!: A Social History of Industrial Unionism in Meatpacking, 1930–90* (Champaign: University of Illinois Press, 1997).

37. The gender pay gaps can be compared using these two sources: http://

ec.europa.eu/eurostat/statistics-explained/index.php/Gender_pay_gap statistics; and http://www.pewresearch.org/fact-tank/2018/04/09/gen-der-pay -gap-facts/.

38. For some evidence of this in the United States, see Steve Early, *Refinery Town: Big Oil, Big Money, and the Remaking of an American City* (Boston: Beacon Press, 2017). For Europe, see Nora Räthzel and David Uzzell, "Trade Unions and Climate Change: The Jobs versus Environment Dilemma," https://www.researchgate.net/publication/234167036_Trade_Unions_and_Climate_Change_The_Jobs_versus_Environment_ Dilemma.

5. The Power of Capital Is Still Intact

1. On this and the importance of political slogans, see Michael D. Yates, "Occupy Wall Street and the Significance of Political Slogans," *Counterpunch*, February 27, 2013, https://www.counterpunch.org/2013/02/27/occupy-wall-street-and-the-significance-of-political -slogans/.

2. On the communes, see William Hinton, *Fanshen: A Documentary of Revolution in a Chinese Village* (New York: Monthly Review Press, 2008), first published in 1966; and Zhun Xu, *From Commune to Capitalism: How China's Peasants Lost Collective Farming and Gained Urban Poverty* (New York: Monthly Review Press, 2018).

3. Paul Le Blanc and Michael D. Yates, *A Freedom Budget for All Americans: Recapturing the Promise of the Civil Rights Movement in the Struggle for Economic Justice Today* (New York: Monthly Review Press. 2013), Kindle edition. This book contains much useful information on the rise of neoliberalism and what might be done to reverse it.

4. For a pointed account of the damage done to Great Britain's working class by years of austerity, see Peter S. Goodman, "In Britain, Austerity Is Changing Everything," *New York Times*, May 28, 2018, https://www.nytimes.com/2018/05/28/world/europe/uk-austerity-poverty.html.

5. An excellent analysis of why the Soviet mode of production could not continue to reproduce itself is Michael A. Lebowitz, *The Contradictions of "Real Socialism": The Conductor and the Conducted* (New York: Monthly Review Press, 2012).

6. Kate Connolly, "German Reunification 25 Years On: How Different Are East and West Really?," *The Guardian*, October 2, 2015, https://www.theguardian.com/world/2015/oct/02/german-reunification-25-years-on-how-different-are-east-and-west-really.

7. Andrea Thomas, "Germany to Cut Public-Sector Investment as Welfare Spending Rises," *Wall Street Journal*, May 2, 2018.

8. Jon Erik Dølvik, *The Nordic Model Towards 2030: A New Chapter?*, http://www.feps-europe.eu/assets/be19fb1f-35a7-4465-9cb2-ca165d-dcfb6a/ 20393-ex-sum-feps.pdf.

9. William Horobin and Nick Kostov, "Macron Law Jolts French Labor Market," *Wall Street Journal*, February 19, 2018. https://www.nytimes. com/2017/03/19/world/europe/europe-neo-fascist-revival-slovakia. html.

10. William Horobin and Nick Kostov, "Macron Outlines Plans to Overhaul France's Labor Laws," *Wall Street Journal*, June 28, 2017.

11. On the situation in Greece, see Helena Sheehan, *The Syriza Wave: Surging and Crashing with the Greek Left* (New York: Monthly Review Press, 2017).

12. The *Week* Staff, "The misery of everyday life in Greece," *The Week*, August 1, 2015, http://theweek.com/articles/569124/misery-everyday -life-greece.

13. For more on how unions have come to behave in ways similar to their adversaries, see Michael D. Yates, *In and Out of the Working Class* (Winnipeg: ARP Books, 2009) and Michael D. Yates, *Why Unions Matter*, second edition (New York: Monthly Review Press, 2009).

14. For a dissident's analysis of the UAW, see Gregg Shotwell, *Autoworkers Under the Gun: A Shop-Floor View of the End of the American Dream* (Chicago: Haymarket Books, 2011), Kindle edition.

15. For union salary data, see https://www.unionfacts.com/.

16. Robert Fitch, *Solidarity for Sale: How Corruption Destroyed the Labor Movement and Undermined America's Promise* (New York: Public Affairs, 2006). See also Michael D. Yates, "What's the Matter with U.S. Organized Labor? An Interview with Robert Fitch," March 30, 2006, https://mronline.org/2006/03/30/whats-the-matter-with-u-s-organized-labor-an-interview-with-robert-fitch/.

17. On the UFW's transformation from an iconic union that organized migrant farmworkers, who were the poorest of the poor, into a quasi-corrupt business operation, see Michael D. Yates, "A Union Is Not a Movement," https://mronline.org/2006/01/16/a-union-is-not-a-move-ment19-november-1977/. This article references a set of essays in the *Los Angeles Times* by Miriam Pawel that are well worth reading. On the UFW, see Miriam Pawel, *The Union of Their Dreams: Power, Hope, and Struggle in Cesar Chavez's Farm Worker Movement* (New York: Bloomsbury Press, 2009); and Frank Bardacke, *Trampling Out the Vintage: Cesar Chávez and the Two Souls of the United Farm Workers* (New York: Verso, 2012).

18. On the accord, see Michael D. Yates, "Who Will Lead the U.S. Working Class?" *Monthly Review* 65/1 (May 2013): 1–16. Also, see Paul Buhle, *Taking Care of Business: Samuel Gompers, George Meany, Lane Kirkland and the Tragedy of American Labor* (New York: Monthly Review Press, 1999); and Kim Moody, *US Labor in Trouble and*

Transition: The Failure of Reform from Above, the Promise of Revival from Below (New York: Verso, 2007).

19.   Gregg Shotwell, *Autoworkers Under the Gun: A Shop-Floor View of the End of the American Dream*, Kindle edition. Shotwell's many examples of the lack of democracy and corruption in the UAW are astonishing.

20.   For data on the weakening of the union impact on wages, benefits, and inequality, see Lawrence Mishel et al., *The State of Working America*, 12th ed. (Ithaca, NY: Cornell University Press, 2012), 268–79.

21.   Heather C. Briccetti and James Cahil, "New Yorkers don't want to pay for single-payer," *Crain's*, June 5, 2018, http://www.crainsnewyork.com/article/20180605/OPINION/180609964/new-yorkers-dont-want-to-pay-for-single-payer.

22.   Benjamin Weinthal, "Where Is the German Trade Union Movement and Where Is It Going?," February 21, 2007, https://mronline.org/2007/02/21/where-is-the-german-trade-union-movement-and-where-is-it-going/.

23.   Asbjørn Wahl, "European Labor: The Ideological Legacy of the Social Pact," *Monthly Review* 55/8 (January 2004): 37–49. Wahl's essay of ten years later shows that little has changed and that, in fact, things may well have gotten worse; see Asbjørn Wahl, "European Labor: Political and Ideological Crisis in an Increasingly More Authoritarian European Union," *Monthly Review* 65/8 (January 2014): 36–57.

24.   On race and gender differences in U.S. unions, see Michael D. Yates, "Race, Gender, Ethnicity, and Sexual Orientation," in *Why Unions Matter* (New York: Monthly Review Press, 2009), Kindle edition.

25.   Michaël Privot, "Trade unions must do more to tackle racial discrimination in Europe's job market," *Equal Times*, https://www.equaltimes.org/trade-unions-must-do-more-to?lang=en#.WwyVx0gvxPY; Dr. Nouria Ouali, "Racism and Discrimination at Work: A Challenge for European Trade Unions," September 10, 2013, https://heimatkunde.boell.de/2013/09/10/racism-and-discrimination-work-challenge-european-trade-unions; Cinzia Sechi, *Women in Trade Unions in Europe: Bridging the Gaps* (Brussels: European Trade Union Confederation, 2007). For a list of reports from the European Trade Union Confederation on gender issues, see https://www.etuc.org/en/issue/gender-equality.

26.   Michael D. Yates, "Hoffa and Trumka Babble While the House of Labor Burns," September 17, 2011, http://cheapmotelsandahotplate.org/2011/09/17/hoffa-and-trumka-babble-while-the-house-of-labor-burns/.

27.   For a useful account of the Corbyn phenomenon, see Richard Seymour, *Corbyn: The Strange Rebirth of Radical Politics* (London: Verso Books, 2016).

28. Asbjørn Wahl, "European Labor: Political and Ideological Crisis in an Increasingly More Authoritarian European Union," 38.
29. Ibid., 36–37.
30. Ibid., 38.
31. On Trump and U.S. fascism, see John Bellamy Foster, *Trump in the White House: Tragedy and Farce* (New York: Monthly Review Press, 2017). On European neo-fascism, see Rick Lyman, "Once in the Shadows, Europe's Neo-Fascists Are Re-emerging," *New York Times*, March 19, 2017, https://www.nytimes.com/2017/03/19/world/europe/europe-neo-fascist-revival-slovakia.html.

6. Can the Working Class Radically Change the World?

1. This and the next seven paragraphs are a revised version of Michael D. Yates, "The 'I' and the 'We,'" May 23, 2010, http://cheapmotelsanda-hotplate.org/2010/05/23/the-i-and-the-we/.
2. John Steinbeck, *The Grapes of Wrath* (London: Penguin Classics, 2006).
3. See, for example, Brian M. Lucey, "Is (Teaching) Economics Doing More Harm than Good?," October 26, 2014, https://brianmlucey.wordpress.com/2014/10/26/is-teaching-economics-doing-more-harm-than-good/.
4. Peter Linebaugh, *Stop, Thief!: The Commons, Enclosures, and Resistance* (Oakland, CA: PM Press, 2013).
5. Ibid.
6. For many examples of what Linebaugh calls "communing," see ibid.
7. Jessica Silver-Greenberg and Shaila Dewan, "When Bail Feels Less Like Freedom, More Like Extortion," *New York Times*, March 31, 2018, https://www.nytimes.com/2018/03/31/us/bail-bonds-extortion.html.
8. Michael D. Yates, "The Growing Degradation of Work and Life, and What We Might Do to End It," *Truthout*, March 21, 2015, https://truthout.org/articles/the-growing-degradation-of-work-and-life-and-what-we-might-do-to-end-it/.
9. Linebaugh, *Stop Thief!*.
10. Yates, "The Growing Degradation of Work and Life, and What We Might Do to End It."
11. James Scofield and Michael Yates, "Teaching Marxists to Teach," *Monthly Review* 30/9 (September 1979): 61–62.
12. Leo Huberman, "How to Spread the Word," *Monthly Review* 19/7 (December 1967): 44–51.
13. Ian Angus, *Facing the Anthropocene: Fossil Capitalism and the Crisis of the Earth System* (New York: Monthly Review Press, 2016), 160.
14. Ibid.
15. Ibid., 159.

16. The lower estimate is from the World Food Program, http://www1.
    wfp.org/zero-hunger, the higher estimate is from Eric Holt-Gimenez,
    *A Foodie's Guide to Capitalism: Understanding the Political Economy
    of What We Eat* (New York: Monthly Review Press, 2017), 178.

17. For a particularly gruesome example of land theft, with perhaps
    500,000 killed, this time in the interest of global mining companies,
    see Gemima Harvey, "The Human Tragedy of West Papua," *The
    Diplomat*, January 15, 2014, https://thediplomat.com/2014/01/
    the-human-tragedy-of-west-papua/.

18. Fred Magdoff, "A Rational Agriculture Is Incompatible with Capitalism,"
    Monthly Review 66/10 (March 2015): 9–11. This essay provided much
    useful information on the social irrationality of market-based agricul-
    ture. In this chapter, I have not discussed fishing, but what has been
    occurring in the oceans is no different than on land. Fishers share the
    same plight as farmers. See Stefano B. Longo, Rebecca Clausen, and
    Brett Clark, *The Tragedy of the Commodity: Oceans, Fisheries, and
    Aquaculture* (New Brunswick, NJ: Rutgers University Press, 2015).

19. This paragraph relies upon the informative essay by economist and
    Latin America expert Sinan Koont. See Sinan Koont, "The Urban
    Agriculture of Havana," *Monthly Review* 60/8 (January 1959): 44–63.

20. On the U.S. blockade of Cuba, see Salim Lamrani, *The Economic
    War Against Cuba: A Historical and Legal Perspective on the U.S.
    Blockade* (New York: Monthly Review Press, 2013).

21. Tom Perkins, "On urban farming and 'colonialism' in Detroit's North
    End neighborhood," *METROTIMES*, December 20, 2017, https://
    www.metrotimes.com/detroit/on-urban-farming-and-colonialism-in-
    detroits-north-end-neighborhood/Content?oid =7950059.

22. Larry Gabriel, "Grace Boggs, Detroit and the Next Revolution,"
    METROTIMES, March 30, 2011, https://www.metrotimes.com/detroit/
    grace-boggs-detroit-and-the-next-revolution/Content?oid=2148354.

23. Ian Frazier, "The Vertical Farm: Growing crops in the city, without soil
    or natural light," *The New Yorker*, January 9, 2017, https://www.newy-
    orker.com/magazine/2017/01/09/the-vertical-farm.

24. Ibid.

25. Jules Pretty, "Can Ecological Agriculture Feed Nine Billion People?"
    Monthly Review 61/6 (November 2009): 46–58.

26. Paul E. Little, "New Large Dams in Amazon Could Lead to Ecosystem
    Collapse," September 5, 2013, https://www.internationalrivers.org/
    resources/new-large-dams-in-amazon-could-lead-to-ecosystem-
    collapse-8081; Tom Gatehouse, ed., *Voices of Latin America: Social
    Movements and the New Activism* (Rugby, UK: Practical Action
    Publishing, forthcoming).

27. For the history of peasant uprisings in India, see Bernard D'Mello, *India After Naxalbari: Unfinished History* (New York: Monthly Review Press, 2018).

28. Eric Holt-Gimenez, *A Foodie's Guide to Capitalism: Understanding the Political Economy of What We Eat*, 111.

29. Benjamin Dangl, "Occupy, Resist, Produce: The Strategy and Political Vision of Brazil's Landless Workers' Movement," *TOWARD FREEDOM*, May 22, 2018, https://towardfreedom.org/archives/americas/occupy-resist-produce-the-strategy-and-political-vision-of-brazils-landless-workers-movement/.

30. Holt-Gimenez, *A Foodie's Guide to Capitalism*, 65.

31. No better book on the difficulties of ridding a union of its entrenched and corrupt leaders can be found than Gregg Shotwell's *Autoworkers Under the Gun: A Shop-Floor View of the End of the American Dream* (Chicago: Haymarket Books, 2011).

32. On the Teamsters, see Dan La Botz, *Rank-and-File Rebellion: Teamsters for a Democratic Union* (Chicago: Haymarket Books, 1991). For the Mineworkers, see Paul F. Clark, *The Miners' Fight for Democracy: Arnold Miller and the Reform of the United Mine Workers* (Ithaca, NY: Cornell University Press, 1981).

33. On the history of two United Electrical Workers locals in a small industrial city, see James Young, *Union Power: The United Electrical Workers in Erie, Pennsylvania* (New York: Monthly Review Press, 2017). See also Michael D. Yates, *Why Unions Matter* (New York: Monthly Review Press, 2009).

34. On European trade unions, see Asbjørn Wahl, "European Labor: Political and Ideological Crisis in an Increasingly More Authoritarian European Union," *Monthly Review* 65/8 (January 2014): 36–57.

35. National Union of Healthcare Workers website: http://nuhw.org/about/.

36. Andreas Malm, "Revolution in a Warming World: Lessons from the Russian to the Syrian Revolutions," http://climateandcapitalism.com/2018/03/17/malm-revolutionary-strategy/.

37. Ibid.

38. Shotwell, *Autoworkers Under the Gun.*

39. Benjamin Dangl, "Occupy, Resist, Produce: The Strategy and Political Vision of Brazil's Landless Workers' Movement."

40. For examples, see Bernard D'Mello, *India After Naxalbari: Unfinished History* (New York: Monthly Review Press, 2018).

41. Michael Zelenko, "Colombian Union Leaders Are Being Hunted by Paramilitary Groups," *Vice News*, April 1, 2014, https://news.vice.com/article/colombian-union-leaders-are-being-hunted-by-paramilitary-groups.

42. Michelle Chen, "Can millennials save unions in America?," *The Guardian*, June 29, 2018, https://www.theguardian.com/world/2018/jun/29/can-millennials-save-unions-in-america.

43. Elly Leary, "Immokalee Workers Take Down Taco Bell," *Monthly Review* 57/5 (October 2005): 21–22. For information on the Chinese Staff & Workers' Association, see http://cswa.org. For a book-length account of worker centers, see Janice Fine, *Worker Centers: Organizing Communities at the Edge of the Dream* (Ithaca, NY: Cornell University Press, 2006).

44. On the Richmond model, see Steve Early, *Refinery Town: Big Oil, Big Money, and the Remaking of an American City* (Boston: Beacon Press, 2017); and Michael D. Yates, "The Promises and Limitations of Radical Local Politics," *Counterpunch*, April 12, 2017, https://www.counterpunch.org/2017/04/12/the-promises-and-limitations-of-radical-local-politics/.

45. Malm, "Revolution in a Warming World."

46. Richard Seymour and Michael D. Yates, "'Mourning and Militancy': Richard Seymour interviewed by Michael D. Yates," *Monthly Review* 68/10 (March 2017): 22.

47. For a vivid account of the struggles of black workers in the steel industry, see the fine film by filmmaker Tony Buba and former black steelworker Ray Henderson, *Struggles in Steel*, available from California Newsreel, http://www.newsreel.org/nav/title.asp?tc=CN0090.

48. For a history of DRUM and related movements, see Dan Georgakis and Marvin Surkin, *Detroit: I Do Mind Dying: A Study in Urban Revolution*, 3rd ed. (Chicago: Haymarket Books, 2012).

49. Michael D. Yates, *The Great Inequality* (London: Routledge, 2016).

50. This and the next paragraph rely heavily on Teresa L. Ebert, "Alexandra Kollontai and Red Love," *Against the Current* 81 (July–August 1999), https://solidarity-us.org/atc/81/p1724/.

51. Esteban Morales Domínguez. *Race in Cuba: Essays on the Revolution and Racial Inequality* (New York: Monthly Review Press, 2013).

52. Ibid.

53. See the discussion of caste in Bernard D'Mello, *India After Naxalbari: Unfinished History*, 321–28. These pages comprise an Appendix to D'Mello's book, and they are must reading for anyone who believes that the issue of race (and in India, caste) will be solved by class-first economic policies.

54. David R. Roediger, *Class, Race, and Marxism* (London: Verso, 2017).

55. For good introductions to the immigration issue, see Jane Guskin and David Wilson, *The Politics of Immigration: Questions and Answers*, 2nd ed. (New York: Monthly Review Press, 2017); and David Bacon, *The Right to Stay Home: How US Policy Drives Mexican Migration* (Boston: Beacon Press, 2013).

56. For some examples of how the United States is treating immigrant children, see Kristine Phillips, "'America is better than this': What a doctor saw in a Texas shelter for migrant children," *Washington Post*, June 16, 2018, https://www.washingtonpost.com/news/post-nation/wp/2018/06/16/america-is-better-than-this-what-a-doctor-saw-in-a-texas-shelter-for-migrant-children/?noredirect=on&utm_term=.be9784dc62ab.

57. On the failure of German labor unions to aggressively support immigrants, see Neva Low, "German Unions and the Rise of Anti-Immigrant Populism," *The Worker Institute*, February 9, 2018, https://www.ilr.cornell.edu/mobilizing-against-inequality/post/german-unions-and-rise-anti-immigrant-populism.

58. For the positive impact of immigrants on the U.S. labor movement, see Jonathan Rosenblum, "How Immigrant Workers Are Reviving the Labor Movement," *The Progressive*, March 25, 2017, http://progressive.org/magazine/how-immigrant-workers-are-reviving-the-labor-movement/.

59. On the efficacy of strikes, see Kim Moody, *On New Terrain: How Capital Is Reshaping the Battleground of Class War* (Chicago: Haymarket Books, 2017). See also Joe Burns, *Reviving the Strike: How Working People Can Regain Power and Transform America* (New York: Ig Publishing, 2011) and Joe Burns, *Strike Back: Using the Militant Tactics of Labor's Past to Reignite Public Sector Unionism Today* (New York: Ig Publishing, 2014).

60. On the *Piquetero* movement, see Moira Birss, "The Piquetero Movement: Organizing for Democracy and Social Change in Argentina's Informal Sector," *Journal of the International Institute* 12/2 (Winter 2005), https://quod.lib.umich.edu/j/jii/4750978.0012.206?view=text;rgn=main; New Compass Collective, "The Fall of the Argentine Assembly Movement," http://new-compass.net/news/fall-argentine-assembly-movement.

61. Nicole D. Nelson, "When Will Black Lives Matter in St. Louis?," *New York Times*, September 20, 2017, https://www.nytimes.com/2017/09/20/opinion/when-will-black-lives-matter-in-st-louis.html; Michael Joseph Roberto, "Crisis, Recovery, and the Transitional Economy: The Struggle for Cooperative Ownership in Greensboro, North Carolina," *Monthly Review* 66/1 (May 2014): 50–60.

62. Joshua Bloom and Waldo E. Martin, Jr., *Black Against Empire: The History and Politics of the Black Panther Party* (Berkeley: University of California Press, 2013).

63. Michael D. Yates, "Occupy Wall Street and the Significance of Political Slogans," *Counterpunch*, February 27, 2013, https://www.counterpunch.org/2013/02/27/occupy-wall-street-and-the-significance-of-political-slogans/.

64. An informative interview with sociologist Dario Azzellini provides much useful information about attempts to build socialism in Venezuela. Ricardo Vaz, "Communes and Workers' Control in Venezuela: Interview with Dario Azzellini," *MR online*, May 2, 2018, https://mronline.org/2018/05/02/communes-and-workers-control-in-venezuela/.

65. Chris Gilbert, "Venezuela's embarrassment of riches?: Socialism is not in a race against capitalism," *MR online*, https://mronline.org/2018/06/25/venezuelas-embarrassment-of-riches/

66. In Ricardo Paz's interview (note 64), Azzellini points out that grassroots efforts to gain working-class control over production and distribution have been occurring throughout the world: "The first internationally visible case was the Zapatista uprising in Chiapas, we saw it in Venezuela like we have been discussing, but also in places like Argentina, Bolivia or even Kurdistan, always in different forms. We saw it in the workplace recuperations that occurred worldwide, we saw it in Occupy Wall Street and 15M, in Gezi and Tahrir, as well as plenty of other cases that we barely heard about, for example in Africa."

67. The discussion of Jackson is based upon Kali Akuno and Ajamu Nangwaya, *Jackson Rising: The Struggle for Economic Democracy and Black Self-Determination in Jackson, Mississippi* (Montreal: Daraja Press, 2017); and Max Ajl, "A Socialist Southern Strategy in Jackson," *Viewpoint Magazine*, June 5, 2018, https://www.viewpointmag.com/2018/06/05/a-socialist-southern-strategy-in-jackson/.

68. Robin D. G. Kelley, "Black Study, Black Struggle," *Boston Review*, March 7, 2016, http://bostonreview.net/forum/robin-d-g-kelley-black-study-black-struggle.

69. Michael D. Yates, "Radical Labor Education, Part 2," January 4, 2011, http://cheapmotelsandahotplate.org/2011/01/04/radical-labor-education-part-2/.

70. Kelley, "Black Study, Black Struggle."

71. Taylor McNeil, "The Mathematics of Inequality," *TuftsNow*, June 10, 2018, http://now.tufts.edu/articles/mathematics-inequality.

72. Singh said this from prison, seven weeks before he was executed. On Singh's life and work, see Chaman Lal, *Understanding Bhagat Singh* (New Delhi: Aakar Books, 2013).

Index